HMH | **into Math**™

Getting Ready for High-Stakes Assessment

Grade 3

Contents

About *Getting Ready for High-Stakes Assessment*

This *Getting Ready for High-Stakes Assessment* print guide consists of standards-based practice and practice tests.

Standards-Based Practice

The items in each practice set are designed to give students exposure to the wide variety of ways in which a standard may be assessed.

All standards-based practice sets are available to students online. Online item types include traditional multiple choice as well as technology-enhanced item types that are similar to the ones students will see on actual high-stakes assessments. The online practice experience also offers students hints, corrective feedback, and opportunities to try an item multiple times. You can assign online standards-based practice and receive instant access to student data and reports. The reports can help you pinpoint student strengths and weaknesses and tailor instruction to meet their needs. The standards-based practice sets in this guide mirror those found online; however, some technology-enhanced item types have been modified or replaced with items suitable for paper-and-pencil testing.

Practice Tests

Into Math also includes three practice tests. The practice tests are available online. Online item types include traditional multiple choice as well as technology-enhanced item types that are similar to ones students will see on actual high-stakes assessments. You can assign the online tests for instant access to data and standards alignments. The practice tests in this guide mirror those found online; however, some technology-enhanced item types were modified or replaced with items suitable for paper-and-pencil testing. This guide includes record forms for these tests that show the content focus and depth of knowledge for each item.

Assessment Item Types

High-stakes assessments contain item types beyond the traditional multiple-choice format. This allows for a more robust assessment of students' understanding of concepts and skills. High-stakes assessments are administered via computers, and *Into Math* presents items in formats similar to what students will see on the real tests. The following information is provided to help you familiarize your students with these different types of items. An example of each item type appears on the following pages. You may want to use the examples to introduce the item types to students. These pages describe the most common item types. You may find other types on some tests.

Example 1: Multiselect

Upon first glance, many students may easily confuse this item type with a traditional multiple-choice item. Explain to students that this type of item will have a special direction line that asks them to select all the answers to the problem that are correct.

What equations does this model show?

Select **all** the correct answers.

Ⓐ 4 × 3 = 12   Ⓓ 12 = 4 × 3

Ⓑ 3 × 4 = 7   Ⓔ 4 × 4 = 16

Ⓒ 7 = 3 × 4

Example 2: Fill in the Blank

Sometimes when students take a digital test, they will have to select a word, number, or symbol from a drop-down list or drag answer options into blanks. The print versions of the *Into Math* tests ask students to write the correct answer in the blank.

Mark's backpack weighs 2,415 g. Lin's backpack weighs 3 kg. How do these masses compare? Write <, >, or = in the blank.

2,415 g _____ 3 kg

Example 3: Classification

Some *Into Math* assessment items require students to categorize numbers or shapes. Digital versions of this item type require students to drag answer options into the correct place in a table. When the classification involves more complex equations or drawings, each object will have a letter next to it. Print versions of this item type will ask students to write answer options in the correct place in the table. Tell students that sometimes they may write the same number or word in more than one column of the table.

Write the name of each quadrilateral into the correct place in the table. Some quadrilaterals may be used more than once or not at all.

Has 2 Pairs of Parallel Sides	Has 4 Congruent Angles

trapezoid   rectangle

square   rhombus

Example 4: Matching

In some items, students will need to match one set of objects to another. In some computer-based items, students will need to drag an answer option into a box next to the element it matches. On paper-based tests, they do this by drawing a line connecting the two elements that match.

Draw a line to match each expression in the left column with an expression in the right column.

4×6	$7 + 7 + 7 + 7$
4×4	$4 + 4 + 4 + 4$
7×4	$7 + 7$
7×2	$4 + 4 + 4 + 4 + 4 + 4$

Example 5: Choice Matrix

Students may also need to match elements by filling in a table. On the digital tests, they select buttons in the table to indicate the correct answers. On paper-based tests, they place X's in the table to indicate the correct answers.

Place an X in the table to show if each fraction is equivalent to 1.

	Yes	No
$\frac{7}{7}$		
$\frac{7}{1}$		
$\frac{1}{1}$		
$\frac{1}{7}$		

Example 6: Graphing/Number Line

On computerized tests, students will be expected to use a graphing tool to plot points, graph lines, and draw polygons. On paper-based versions of these items, students will plot, graph, or draw on a grid or number line supplied with the item.

Lea's backpack weighs 3 pounds. José's backpack weighs $3\frac{1}{2}$ pounds. Cora's backpack weighs more than Lea's backpack but less than José's.

Plot a point on the number line to show the weight of Cora's backpack.

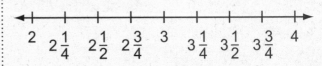

Example 7: Shading

Shading items allow students to select boxes to shade portions of an interactive rectangular array. In the print versions of these items, students shade a model to show the relationship being assessed.

Shade $\frac{1}{3}$ of the whole model.

1 Ms. Rourke divided her class into 2 groups. Each group had 8 students.

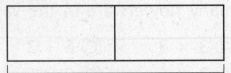

Students

How many students are in Ms. Rourke's class in all?

Ⓐ 4
Ⓑ 10
Ⓒ 14
Ⓓ 16

2 Alan has 2 boxes for his books. He places 7 books in each box. Which equations show the total number of books in Alan's boxes?

Select **all** the correct answers.

Ⓐ $9 = 2 + 7$
Ⓑ $14 = 7 + 7$
Ⓒ $14 = 2 \times 7$
Ⓓ $14 = 2 + 7$
Ⓔ $49 = 7 \times 7$

3 Alondra makes 4 necklaces. She uses 5 beads on each necklace. Which expression could be used to find the number of beads Alondra uses?

Ⓐ 4×5
Ⓑ $5 + 4$
Ⓒ $4 + 4 + 4 + 4$
Ⓓ $5 + 5 + 5 + 5 + 5$

4 Samantha was doing her math homework. She wrote:

$9 + 9 + 9 + 9$

Which is another way to show what Samantha wrote?

Ⓐ 4×4
Ⓑ 9×3
Ⓒ $9 + 4$
Ⓓ 4×9

5 Mr. Jones has 6 baskets with 5 dinner rolls in each basket. How many dinner rolls does he have?

_____ dinner rolls

Name _____

6 Jorge puts 42 stamps in a rectangular array.

Select **all** the sentences that could describe Jorge's array.

Ⓐ Jorge makes 4 rows of 2 stamps.

Ⓑ Jorge makes 40 rows of 2 stamps.

Ⓒ Jorge makes 6 rows of 7 stamps.

Ⓓ Jorge makes 2 rows of 4 stamps.

Ⓔ Jorge makes 7 rows of 6 stamps.

7 Kara uses this expression to find how many oranges are in 4 bags.

$7 + 7 + 7 + 7$

Which of these expressions has the same value?

Ⓐ 4×7 Ⓒ $7 + 4$

Ⓑ 7×7 Ⓓ 4×4

8 The library has 5 tables. There are 4 children sitting at each table. How many children are sitting at the tables?

_____ children

9 Sara has 3 vases. She puts 6 flowers in each vase.

Which expression shows how many flowers are in the vases?

Ⓐ 3×3 Ⓒ $6 + 3$

Ⓑ 3×6 Ⓓ 6×6

10 There are 4 gardens in Max's yard. In each garden, there are 3 rosebushes. How many rosebushes are there?

_____ rosebushes

11 Carlos spent 5 minutes working on each of 8 math problems. Which equation shows the total number of minutes Carlos spent on math problems?

Ⓐ $7 + 6 = 13$

Ⓑ $5 + 8 = 13$

Ⓒ $5 \times 8 = 40$

Ⓓ $8 \times 8 = 64$

1 Amir gets 3 magnets on each of his vacations. He has 9 magnets from his vacations. How many vacations has Amir gone on?

Ⓐ 3
Ⓑ 4
Ⓒ 6
Ⓓ 12

2 Gina has 16 framed pictures of sports stars. She places an equal number of pictures on each of 4 shelves in her room.

How many pictures of sports stars are on each shelf?

Ⓐ 2
Ⓑ 4
Ⓒ 6
Ⓓ 8

3 A book has 54 pages divided into 6 equal chapters. How many pages are in each chapter?

There are _____ pages in each chapter.

4 Marcel has 20 postcards from his trips. He got 4 postcards from each of his trips. How many trips has Marcel gone on?

Ⓐ 5
Ⓑ 8
Ⓒ 16
Ⓓ 24

5 Max writes a total of 45 lines in his journal. Each journal entry is 9 lines long. How many journal entries does Max write?

Max writes _____ journal entries.

Name _____

6 Wu has 18 trophies. She places an equal number of trophies on each of 3 shelves in her room.

How many trophies are on each shelf?

Ⓐ 2 Ⓒ 6
Ⓑ 4 Ⓓ 9

7 Carson earns $6 for each hour that he babysits. Last week, he earned a total of $48 for babysitting. How many hours did Carson babysit last week?

Carson babysat for _____ hours last week.

8 Todd has 12 seashells from his trips to the beach. He puts 3 seashells in each jar. How many jars does Todd need to display all his seashells?

Ⓐ 4 Ⓒ 9
Ⓑ 8 Ⓓ 36

9 Elian is making 36 ounces of punch. He pours the same amount into each of 6 cups. How many ounces of punch does he pour into each cup?

Elian pours _____ ounces of punch into each cup.

10 Brad has 15 model cars. He places an equal number of model cars onto 3 shelves.

How many model cars are on each shelf?

Ⓐ 3 Ⓒ 6
Ⓑ 5 Ⓓ 8

1 Anh arranges 72 coins into
9 equal groups.

How many coins are in each
group?

Ⓐ 9   Ⓒ 6

Ⓑ 8   Ⓓ 4

---

2 Eamon uses 4 buttons on each
sock puppet. How many
buttons does he need for
7 sock puppets?

Ⓐ 3   Ⓒ 11

Ⓑ 7   Ⓓ 28

---

3 Topher buys 2 packages
of water bottles. There
are 3 bottles in each
package.

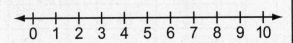

How many water bottles does
Topher buy in all?

Ⓐ 1   Ⓒ 6

Ⓑ 5   Ⓓ 23

4 At a dance class, the teacher
divided the class into 2 groups.
Each group had 7 students.

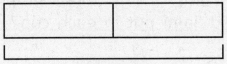

Students

How many students were
there in all?

Ⓐ 5   Ⓒ 14

Ⓑ 9   Ⓓ 18

---

5 Rachel drew an array to show
the number of stamps on a
page in her scrapbook.

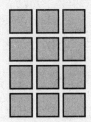

Which shows the total number
of stamps on a page in
Rachel's scrapbook?

Ⓐ $3 \times 4 = 7$

Ⓑ $3 \times 4 = 12$

Ⓒ $4 \times 4 = 16$

Ⓓ $3 \times 4 = 34$

6 Sami divided 56 grapes into 7 small cups for his friends. Each cup has the same number of grapes. How many grapes did Sami put in each cup?

$56 \div 7 = \triangle$

$7 \times \triangle = 56$

Ⓐ 6   Ⓒ 49

Ⓑ 8   Ⓓ 63

7 Tyrone took 16 pennies from his bank and put them in 4 equal stacks.

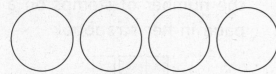

How many pennies were in each stack?

_____

8 There are 7 cars in an amusement park ride. There are 42 people on the ride with an equal number of people in each car.

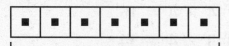

42 People

How many people are in each car?

_____

9 There were 40 fingers on the gloves Mr. Edwards knitted. If there are 5 fingers on each glove, how many gloves did he knit?

40 Fingers

_____

10 Chris plants 40 pumpkin seeds in 5 equal rows. How many pumpkin seeds does he plant in each row?

Shade the model to show how many seeds are in each row.

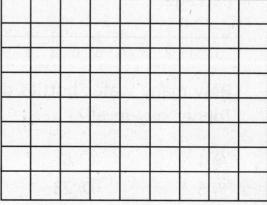

1 What is the value of the unknown number?

$6 \times ? = 42$

Ⓐ 6   Ⓒ 8

Ⓑ 7   Ⓓ 9

2 What is the value of the unknown number?

$56 \div 7 = ?$

Ⓐ 6   Ⓒ 8

Ⓑ 7   Ⓓ 9

3 Place an X in the table to show if 9 is the unknown factor in each equation.

	Yes	No
$6 \times ? = 56$		
$? \times 4 = 42$		
$8 \times ? = 72$		
$? \times 5 = 45$		

4 What is the value of the unknown number?

$? \div 9 = 6$

Ⓐ 36   Ⓒ 54

Ⓑ 45   Ⓓ 56

5 What is the value of the unknown number?

$64 \div \underline{\quad\quad} = 8$

6 What is the value of the unknown number?

$81 \div ? = 9$

Ⓐ 6   Ⓒ 8

Ⓑ 7   Ⓓ 9

---

7 Fill in the blanks with the correct numbers from the list to complete the unknown factor problems. You will not use all the numbers.

$24 \div$ _____ $= 4$

$24 \div$ _____ $= 3$

| 3 | 4 | 6 | 8 |

_____ $\times 4 = 12$

---

8 What is the value of the unknown number?

$3 \times ? = 24$

Ⓐ 4   Ⓒ 8

Ⓑ 6   Ⓓ 10

---

9 Select **all** of the equations in which the unknown factor is even.

Ⓐ $2 \times ? = 14$

Ⓑ $3 \times ? = 24$

Ⓒ $4 \times ? = 24$

Ⓓ $5 \times ? = 35$

Ⓔ $7 \times ? = 56$

Ⓕ $8 \times ? = 64$

---

10 What is the value of the unknown number?

$9 \times ? = 18$

Ⓐ 2   Ⓒ 6

Ⓑ 3   Ⓓ 8

8

1 Which number sentence is related to $3 \times 6 = 18$?

Ⓐ $6 \times 3 = \square$

Ⓑ $6 + 3 = \square$

Ⓒ $3 + 3 + 3 = \square$

Ⓓ $6 \times 6 = \square$

2 Which number sentence shows the Commutative Property of Multiplication?

Ⓐ $5 \times 2 = 5 + 5$

Ⓑ $6 \times 0 = 0$

Ⓒ $7 \times 5 = 5 \times 7$

Ⓓ $9 \times 1 = 9$

3 Select **all** the number sentences that show the Commutative Property of Multiplication.

Ⓐ $3 \times 2 = 2 \times 3$

Ⓑ $4 \times 9 = 4 \times 9$

Ⓒ $5 \times 0 = 0$

Ⓓ $6 \times 1 = 1 \times 6$

Ⓔ $7 \times 2 = 14 \times 1$

4 Which expression is equal to 9×4?

Ⓐ $4 + (5 \times 4)$

Ⓑ $5 + (4 \times 5)$

Ⓒ $4 \times (5 + 4)$

Ⓓ $5 \times (4 + 5)$

Name _____

5 Draw a line from each expression to its quotient.

$5 \div 5$ •	•	0
$0 \div 5$ •	•	5
$5 \div 1$ •	•	1

6 Which number sentence has the same value as 7×5?

Ⓐ $7 + (3 + 2) = \blacksquare$

Ⓑ $7 \times (3 + 2) = \blacksquare$

Ⓒ $(5 \times 2) + (5 \times 3) = \blacksquare$

Ⓓ $(7 \times 2) + (7 \times 5) = \blacksquare$

7 Which number makes the sentence true?

The product of any number and _____ is zero.

8 Which equation is true?

Ⓐ $5 \div 1 = 1$

Ⓑ $5 \div 5 = 1$

Ⓒ $3 \div 1 = 1$

Ⓓ $0 \div 1 = 1$

9 Which number makes the equation true?

$7 \div 1 =$ _____

10 Which number completes the equation $0 \div 7 = \blacksquare$?

Ⓐ 0

Ⓑ 1

Ⓒ 7

Ⓓ 14

1 Which multiplication fact can be used to find the quotient of
$24 \div 4 = n$?

Ⓐ $2 \times 4 = 8$
Ⓑ $3 \times 2 = 6$
Ⓒ $3 \times 8 = 24$
Ⓓ $4 \times 6 = 24$

2 $36 \div 9 = ?$

Which multiplication fact can be used to find the quotient?

Ⓐ $2 \times 9 = 18$
Ⓑ $3 \times 6 = 18$
Ⓒ $4 \times 9 = 36$
Ⓓ $6 \times 6 = 36$

3 $42 \div 6 = ?$

Complete the related multiplication fact to help you divide.

$6 \times$ _____ $= 42$

4 $40 \div 8 = ?$

Which multiplication fact can be used to find the unknown
quotient?

Ⓐ $2 \times 10 = 20$
Ⓑ $4 \times 5 = 20$
Ⓒ $4 \times 10 = 40$
Ⓓ $5 \times 8 = 40$

5 $15 \div 5 = ?$

Complete the related multiplication fact to help you divide.

$5 \times$ _____ $= 15$

6 30 ÷ 3 = ?

Which multiplication fact can be used to find the unknown quotient?

(A) 2 × 5 = 10
(B) 3 × 5 = 15
(C) 3 × 10 = 30
(D) 5 × 6 = 30

---

7 27 ÷ 3 = ?

Complete the related multiplication fact to help you divide.

3 × _____ = 27

---

8 20 ÷ 5 = ?

Which multiplication fact can be used to find the unknown quotient?

(A) 2 × 5 = 10
(B) 2 × 10 = 20
(C) 4 × 5 = 20
(D) 5 × 1 = 5

---

9 Draw a line from each division expression to the multiplication expression that can help you solve it.

49 ÷ 7	●		●	3 × 8
32 ÷ 8	●		●	6 × 4
24 ÷ 6	●		●	7 × 7
24 ÷ 3	●		●	8 × 4

---

10 18 ÷ 3 = ?

Which multiplication fact can be used to find the unknown quotient?

(A) 2 × 3 = 6   (C) 3 × 3 = 9
(B) 2 × 9 = 18   (D) 3 × 6 = 18

1 $3 \times 7 = 21$

$n \times 7 = 35$

What is the value of n?

Ⓐ 3   Ⓒ 7

Ⓑ 5   Ⓓ 14

3 Fill in the blanks with the correct answers to complete the equations.

$4 \times$ _____ $= 24$

_____ $= 24 \div 4$

2 Solve.

$48 \div 6 =$ ■

Ⓐ 5   Ⓒ 7

Ⓑ 6   Ⓓ 8

4 Which expression can be used to find the value of n?

$72 \div n = 8$

Ⓐ 8×6 Ⓒ 8×9

Ⓑ 8×8 Ⓓ 8×10

5 Place an X in the table to show whether each equation is true or false.

	True	False
$0 \div 6 = 6$		
$6 \div 6 = 1$		
$18 \div 6 = 2$		
$54 \div 6 = 9$		
$60 \div 6 = 10$		

6 Which multiplication fact can be used to find the answer to 36 ÷ 4?

(A) 18 × 2 = 36

(B) 12 × 3 = 36

(C) 6 × 6 = 36

(D) 4 × 9 = 36

7 Place an X in the table to show whether each equation is true or false.

	True	False
18 ÷ 9 = 2		
27 ÷ 9 = 4		
45 ÷ 9 = 5		
81 ÷ 9 = 8		

8 Find the quotient.

32 ÷ 4 = ■

(A) 6   (C) 9

(B) 8   (D) 10

9 What is the unknown factor in the equation?

3 × ■ = 24

10 Solve.

24 ÷ 2 = ■

(A) 4   (C) 8

(B) 6   (D) 12

1 Salim has 5 boxes of paint jars. Each box has the same number of paint jars. His teacher gives him 6 more paint jars. Now he has 41 paint jars. How many paint jars were in each box?

Ⓐ 6   Ⓒ 35
Ⓑ 7   Ⓓ 52

2 The table shows the number of bottles Mrs. Green's class recycled each week.

Bottles Recycled

Week	Number of Bottles
Week 1	70
Week 2	45
Week 3	60

The class has a goal of recycling 250 bottles by the end of week 4. How many bottles must they recycle in week 4 to meet that goal?

3 Juan has 3 packages of markers. Each package has the same number of markers. His sister gives him 4 more markers. Now he has 28 markers. How many markers were in each package?

Ⓐ 7   Ⓒ 32
Ⓑ 8   Ⓓ 35

4 Anna's mom makes 3 sandwiches every school day. Each sandwich gets 3 slices of cheese. How many slices of cheese will Anna's mom need for all the sandwiches she makes on 2 school days?

5 Kwan has 4 boxes of crayons. Each box has the same number of crayons. He lost 5 crayons. Now he has 23 crayons. How many crayons were in each box?

Ⓐ 7   Ⓒ 28
Ⓑ 9   Ⓓ 32

6 Mina collects fossils. She has 7 cases of fossils and the same number of fossils in each case. She brings 6 fossils in to show to her class and leaves 43 fossils at home. How many fossils does Mina have altogether?

Ⓐ 37   Ⓒ 49

Ⓑ 43   Ⓓ 55

7 Hudson and Asher each collect comic books. Hudson can arrange his comics into 3 piles with 7 books in each pile. Asher has 8 comic books in his collection. How many comic books do they have in all?

_____

8 For a class picnic, Ms. Key buys 4 boxes of oranges from a local farmer. There are 6 oranges in each box. The students sit at 8 tables. Ms. Key puts the same number of oranges on each table. How many oranges does she put on each table?

Ⓐ 8   Ⓒ 3

Ⓑ 5   Ⓓ 2

9 Carly bought 3 packs of baseball cards. Each pack had the same number of cards. She gave 5 cards to her sister. Now she has 22 cards. How many cards were in each pack?

_____

10 Maria's family set a goal to see how far they could walk in 8 days. Maria walked 2 miles a day for 8 days. Her family walked a total of 57 miles. How many miles did the rest of the family walk?

Ⓐ 41   Ⓒ 67

Ⓑ 47   Ⓓ 73

1 Which of these describes a pattern shown in the table?

2	3	4	5	6
6	9	12	15	18

Ⓐ Add 6

Ⓑ Add 12

Ⓒ Multiply by 3

Ⓓ Multiply by 6

2 The second row in the table describes the product of a one-digit factor and each number in the first row.

X	1	2	3	4	☐
?	odd	even	odd	even	odd

What numbers could replace the question mark to make this pattern work?

Select **all** the correct answers.

Ⓐ 3   Ⓓ 6

Ⓑ 4   Ⓔ 7

Ⓒ 5

3 Which of these describes a pattern shown in the table?

2	3	4	5	6
10	15	20	25	30

Ⓐ Add 10

Ⓑ Add 20

Ⓒ Multiply by 3

Ⓓ Multiply by 5

4 The diagram shows part of a multiplication table.

28	32
35	

What is the missing number?

_____

5 Which of these describes a pattern shown in the table?

2	3	4	5	6
16	24	32	40	48

Ⓐ Add 8

Ⓑ Add 12

Ⓒ Multiply by 6

Ⓓ Multiply by 8

6 Which sum is even?

Ⓐ 8 + 3   Ⓒ 4 + 5

Ⓑ 6 + 6   Ⓓ 2 + 7

7 What is true about sums of odd numbers?

Fill in the blanks with the correct answers from the lists.

The sum of 3 odd numbers is always _____.

even   odd

An example is the 3 numbers _____, which add up to _____.

2, 3, and 5	10
1, 4, and 7	12
1, 3, and 9	13

8 Which pattern can be used to complete the table?

1	2	3	4	5	6
6	12	18			

Ⓐ Add 1

Ⓑ Add 5

Ⓒ Multiply by 2

Ⓓ Multiply by 6

9 Sandra is looking at patterns in the multiplication table. She is finding different ways to write 4 × 8. Which equations are correct?

Select **all** the correct equations.

Ⓐ 4 × 8 = (1 × 1) + (4 × 7)

Ⓑ 4 × 8 = (1 × 1) + (4 × 8)

Ⓒ 4 × 8 = (4 × 1) + (4 × 7)

Ⓓ 4 × 8 = (4 × 1) + (4 × 8)

Ⓔ 4 × 8 = (4 × 4) + (4 × 4)

1 What is the value of 376 rounded to the nearest ten?

(A) 300   (C) 380

(B) 370   (D) 400

---

2 Which numbers equal 500 when rounded to the nearest hundred?

Select **all** the correct answers.

(A) 438

(B) 450

(C) 483

(D) 542

(E) 567

---

3 Which number rounds to 300 when rounded to the
nearest hundred?

(A) 238   (C) 342

(B) 249   (D) 359

---

4 What is the value of 165 rounded to the nearest ten?

_____

---

5 When rounded to the nearest hundred, which number rounds to
100?

(A) 38   (C) 162

(B) 83   (D) 190

---

6 What is 54 rounded to the nearest ten?

(A) 40   (C) 60

(B) 50   (D) 100

Name _____

7 Select the correct original numbers from the list and write them in the table. You will not use all the numbers in the list.

Original Number	Rounded to Nearest Ten
	210
	220
	240

| 209 | 224 | 228 | 233 | 238 |

8 What is 148 rounded to the nearest ten?

Ⓐ 100   Ⓒ 150

Ⓑ 140   Ⓓ 200

9 Do the numbers in the list round to 500 or 600 when rounded to the nearest hundred?

Write each number from the list in the appropriate column in the table.

Rounds to 500	Rounds to 600

| 509 | 520 | 591 | 549 | 550 |

10 Which number rounds to 250 when rounded to the nearest ten and 300 when rounded to the nearest hundred?

Ⓐ 247   Ⓒ 268

Ⓑ 253   Ⓓ 326

1 What is the sum of 547 and 236?

Ⓐ 311
Ⓑ 773
Ⓒ 783
Ⓓ 790

2 $856 - 758 = n$

What is the value of n?

_____

3 $879 - 346 = ?$

Which number sentence can be used to find the difference using place value?

Ⓐ $(8 - 3) + (7 - 4) + (9 - 6) = ?$
Ⓑ $(800 - 300) - (70 - 40) - (9 - 6) = ?$
Ⓒ $(800 - 300) + (70 - 40) + (9 - 6) = ?$
Ⓓ $(900 - 600) + (80 - 30) + (7 - 4) = ?$

4 $682 - 399 = n$

Fill in the blanks to correctly rewrite the subtraction equation as an addition equation, and find the solution to the equation.

_____ $+ n =$ _____

$n =$ _____

5 $525 + 375 = n$

What is the value of n?

Ⓐ 150
Ⓑ 800
Ⓒ 890
Ⓓ 900

Name

6 Which of the following is NOT a way to rewrite the problem $695 - 205 = n$?

(A) $205 + n = 695$

(B) $295 - n = 695$

(C) $695 - 200 - 5 = n$

(D) $(600 - 200) + (90 - 0) + (5 - 5) = n$

7 $273 + 527 = n$

Select **all** the correct ways to rewrite the given equation.

(A) $n - 273 = 527$

(B) $527 - n = 273$

(C) $500 + 200 + 100 = n$

(D) $(500 + 200) + (70 + 20) + 10 = n$

(E) $(200 + 70 + 3) + (500 + n) = (20 + 7)$

8 $977 - 288 = ?$

What is the difference between the numbers?

(A) 689

(B) 699

(C) 711

(D) 799

9 $421 - 295 = n$

What is the value of n?

10 How can you rewrite $144 - 120 = n$ as an addition problem?

(A) $120 + n = 144$

(B) $144 + n = 120$

(C) $(100 + 100) + (40 + 20) + (4 + 0) = n$

(D) $(100 - 100) + (40 + 20) + (4 - 0) = n$

1 Each after-school soccer team has 20 players. There are 6 teams in the after-school program. How many players are there in all?

Ⓐ 26   Ⓑ 120   Ⓒ 122   Ⓓ 1,200

2 Each bus can carry 30 people. How many people can 4 buses carry?

The buses can carry _____ people.

3 Jenna's goal is to learn 8 new words every day. At the end of day 30, how many new words will Jenna have learned?

Ⓐ 38   Ⓑ 160   Ⓒ 240   Ⓓ 2,400

4 Carmen keeps her card collection in a folder with 20 pages. Each page has 8 cards. Willie has 150 cards in his collection.

Select **all** the correct statements.

Ⓐ Carmen has 28 cards.

Ⓑ Carmen has 160 cards.

Ⓒ Carmen has more cards than Willie.

Ⓓ Carmen has fewer cards than Willie.

Ⓔ Carmen has the same number of cards as Willie.

5 A store sells T-shirts for $30 each. Mr. Sanderson buys 7 T-shirts for his children. How much does Mr. Sanderson spend in all on the T-shirts?

Ⓐ $37   Ⓒ $270

Ⓑ $210   Ⓓ $2,100

6 The coach buys 5 new baseball mitts. Each mitt costs $20. What is the total cost of the mitts?

Ⓐ $15   Ⓒ $100

Ⓑ $25   Ⓓ $1,000

Name _____

7 Neil makes this multiplication model. Complete the equation that represents the model.

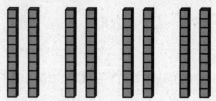

4 × _____ = _____

8 Mr. Marshall buys 3 gift cards to the electronics shop. Each gift card is worth $40. What is the total cost of the 3 gift cards?

Ⓐ $43

Ⓑ $80

Ⓒ $90

Ⓓ $120

9 The bookstore has 6 shelves of books about animals. There are 30 books on each shelf. How many books about animals does the bookstore have?

The bookstore has _____ books about animals.

10 An elephant can drink about 40 gallons of water in a day. How many gallons of water can an elephant drink in 5 days?

Ⓐ 20

Ⓑ 45

Ⓒ 200

Ⓓ 400

1 What fraction of this shape is shaded?

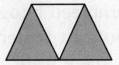

Ⓐ $\frac{3}{3}$ Ⓒ $\frac{3}{2}$

Ⓑ $\frac{2}{3}$ Ⓓ $\frac{3}{1}$

2 The shaded part of the model shows the part of a garden that is planted with peas.

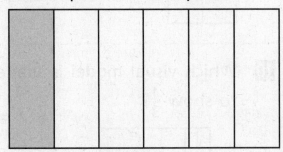

What fraction names the shaded part?

3 Alana divided a garden equally into 4 parts. She planted seeds in 3 of the parts. In what fraction of the garden did Alana plant seeds?

Ⓐ $\frac{1}{4}$ Ⓒ $\frac{3}{4}$

Ⓑ $\frac{1}{3}$ Ⓓ $\frac{4}{3}$

4 What fraction of the circle is shaded?

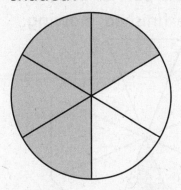

5 What fraction of this circle is shaded?

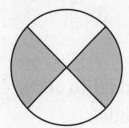

Ⓐ $\frac{2}{4}$

Ⓑ $\frac{2}{2}$

Ⓒ $\frac{4}{4}$

Ⓓ $\frac{4}{2}$

6 Omar shaded the model to show the part of the lawn that he finished mowing.

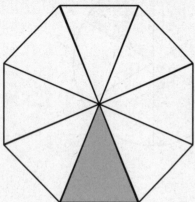

What fraction names the shaded part?

Ⓐ $\frac{1}{8}$ Ⓒ $\frac{5}{6}$

Ⓑ $\frac{1}{6}$ Ⓓ $\frac{7}{8}$

7 Shade the model to show $\frac{5}{8}$ of the whole model.

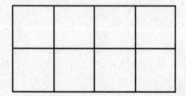

8 Tyra sliced a pizza into 8 equal parts. She ate 2 slices of pizza. What fraction of the pizza did Tyra eat?

Ⓐ $\frac{1}{8}$ Ⓒ $\frac{6}{8}$

Ⓑ $\frac{2}{8}$ Ⓓ $\frac{8}{2}$

9 Jayson baked a pan of cornbread for a family dinner. He cut the cornbread into equal size pieces. At the end of the dinner, there were 2 pieces left.

Shade the model to show the fraction of the cornbread that was eaten.

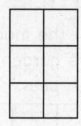

10 Which visual model is shaded to show $\frac{1}{3}$?

Ⓐ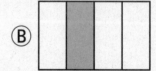

Ⓑ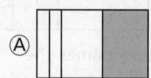

Ⓒ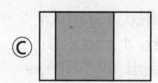

Ⓓ

1 What is the size of the part from 0 to *A*?

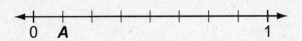

(A) $\frac{1}{2}$ (B) $\frac{1}{4}$ (C) $\frac{1}{6}$ (D) $\frac{1}{8}$

2 How many equal parts should be shown on the number line to represent the fraction $\frac{1}{2}$?

_____ equal parts

3 What fraction names *A* on the number line?

(A) $\frac{1}{3}$ (B) $\frac{1}{4}$ (C) $\frac{1}{6}$ (D) $\frac{1}{8}$

4 Plot a point at $\frac{1}{6}$ on the number line.

5 How many equal parts are shown on the number line?

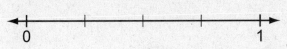

(A) 2 (B) 3 (C) 4 (D) 8

Name _____

6 What fraction names *A* on the number line?

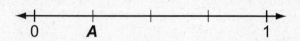

0   *A*   1

Ⓐ $\frac{1}{2}$ Ⓑ $\frac{1}{3}$ Ⓒ $\frac{1}{4}$ Ⓓ $\frac{1}{8}$

---

7 Plot a point at $\frac{1}{3}$ on the number line.

0   1

---

8 Which describes the whole shown on the number line?

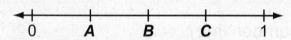

0   *A*   *B*   *C*   1

Ⓐ the part from 0 to *A*
Ⓑ the part from 0 to *B*
Ⓒ the part from 0 to *C*
Ⓓ the part from 0 to 1

---

9 Plot the fraction $\frac{1}{8}$ on the number line.

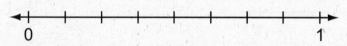

0   1

---

10 How many equal parts should be shown on the number line to represent sixths?

Ⓐ 2   Ⓑ 3   Ⓒ 4   Ⓓ 6

1 Which of the following fractions names the point shown on the number line?

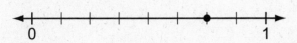

- Ⓐ $\frac{2}{8}$
- Ⓑ $\frac{6}{8}$
- Ⓒ $\frac{7}{9}$
- Ⓓ $\frac{8}{6}$

2 What fraction names point A on the number line?

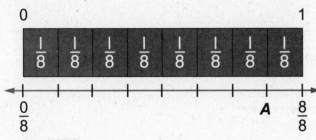

$A = \frac{\square}{8}$

3 What fraction names the point on the number line?

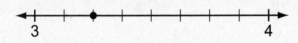

- Ⓐ $\frac{2}{8}$
- Ⓑ $\frac{6}{8}$
- Ⓒ $3\frac{2}{8}$
- Ⓓ $4\frac{6}{8}$

4 Plot a point at $\frac{2}{4}$ on the number line.

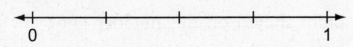

5 Which fraction names the point shown on the number line?

- Ⓐ $\frac{1}{6}$
- Ⓑ $\frac{2}{6}$
- Ⓒ $\frac{1}{2}$
- Ⓓ $\frac{2}{3}$

Name _____

6 Which of the following number lines displays a point at $\frac{2}{3}$?

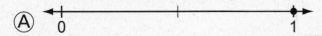

Ⓐ

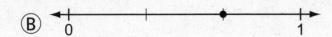

Ⓑ

Ⓒ

Ⓓ

---

7 Plot the points $\frac{1}{6}$ on the number line.

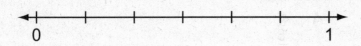

---

8 Which of the following fractions is plotted on the number line?

Ⓐ $\frac{3}{8}$ Ⓑ $\frac{4}{4}$ Ⓒ $\frac{4}{8}$ Ⓓ $\frac{8}{4}$

---

9 Plot a point at $\frac{3}{2}$ on the number line.

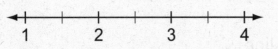

---

10 Which fraction names the point shown on this number line?

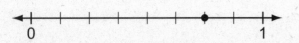

Ⓐ $\frac{2}{8}$ Ⓑ $\frac{3}{8}$ Ⓒ $\frac{6}{8}$ Ⓓ $\frac{7}{8}$

1 The model is shaded to show the fraction $\frac{3}{4}$.

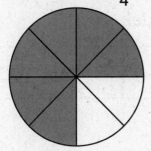

Which fraction is equivalent to $\frac{3}{4}$?

Ⓐ $\frac{3}{8}$ Ⓒ $\frac{5}{8}$

Ⓑ $\frac{4}{8}$ Ⓓ $\frac{6}{8}$

2 The model is shaded to show the fraction $\frac{2}{3}$.

Write a fraction that is equal to $\frac{2}{3}$.

$\frac{2}{3} = $ _____

3 The model is shaded to show the fraction $\frac{1}{2}$.

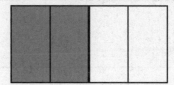

Which fraction is equivalent to $\frac{1}{2}$?

Ⓐ $\frac{1}{4}$ Ⓒ $\frac{3}{4}$

Ⓑ $\frac{2}{4}$ Ⓓ $\frac{4}{4}$

4 It took Mike $\frac{2}{6}$ of an hour to clean his room. What fraction is equivalent to $\frac{2}{6}$?

_____

5 Which fraction makes the equation true?

$\frac{1}{2} = ?$

Ⓐ $\frac{1}{6}$ Ⓒ $\frac{3}{6}$

Ⓑ $\frac{2}{6}$ Ⓓ $\frac{4}{6}$

Name _____

6 The number lines each show a fraction.

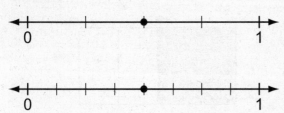

Which fraction is equal to $\frac{2}{4}$?

Ⓐ $\frac{2}{8}$ Ⓒ $\frac{6}{8}$

Ⓑ $\frac{4}{8}$ Ⓓ $\frac{8}{8}$

7 Shade the model to show a fraction equivalent to $\frac{1}{2}$ of the whole model.

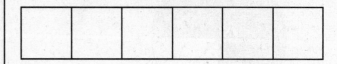

8 Mrs. Smith decorated $\frac{1}{3}$ of her classroom with science posters. Which fraction is equivalent to $\frac{1}{3}$?

Ⓐ $\frac{1}{6}$ Ⓒ $\frac{3}{6}$

Ⓑ $\frac{2}{6}$ Ⓓ $\frac{4}{6}$

9 Shade the model to show a fraction equivalent to $\frac{3}{4}$.

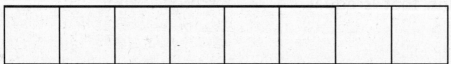

10 Which fraction is equivalent to $\frac{1}{4}$?

Ⓐ $\frac{1}{8}$ Ⓒ $\frac{6}{8}$

Ⓑ $\frac{2}{8}$ Ⓓ $\frac{8}{8}$

1 Nathan makes a design with small squares. He wants $\frac{3}{6}$ of the squares to be red.

Which fraction is equivalent to $\frac{3}{6}$?

Ⓐ $\frac{3}{4}$ Ⓒ $\frac{1}{3}$

Ⓑ $\frac{1}{2}$ Ⓓ $\frac{1}{4}$

2 Shade $\frac{1}{3}$ of the whole model.

3 Which fraction is equivalent to $\frac{6}{8}$?

Ⓐ $\frac{3}{8}$ Ⓒ $\frac{3}{4}$

Ⓑ $\frac{3}{6}$ Ⓓ $\frac{3}{2}$

4 Dalton rode his skateboard for $\frac{3}{4}$ of a mile. Amelia rode hers for an equal distance.

Shade the model to show a fraction equivalent to $\frac{3}{4}$.

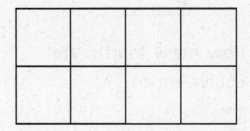

5 Regina used $\frac{1}{2}$ of her pack of craft paper with her friends. There were 6 sheets.

How many sixths of the pack of craft paper did she use with her friends?

Ⓐ 1   Ⓒ 3

Ⓑ 2   Ⓓ 6

6 Which fraction is equivalent to $\frac{2}{3}$?

Ⓐ $\frac{1}{2}$ Ⓒ $\frac{3}{4}$

Ⓑ $\frac{2}{6}$ Ⓓ $\frac{4}{6}$

Name _____

7 Which fraction is equivalent
to $\frac{1}{4}$?

   (A) $\frac{1}{2}$ (C) $\frac{3}{6}$

   (B) $\frac{2}{8}$ (D) $\frac{4}{3}$

8 How many fourths are
equivalent to $\frac{6}{6}$?

$\frac{}{4}$

9 Which fraction is equivalent
to $\frac{4}{8}$?

Select **all** the correct answers.

   (A) $\frac{8}{4}$ (D) $\frac{3}{4}$

   (B) $\frac{1}{2}$ (E) $\frac{3}{6}$

   (C) $\frac{2}{6}$

10 What fraction is equivalent
to $\frac{4}{6}$?

Plot the point on the number
line that is equivalent to $\frac{4}{6}$.

11 Two sisters shared a salad.
Pensri ate $\frac{4}{8}$ of the salad.
Which fraction is equivalent
to $\frac{4}{8}$?

   (A) $\frac{1}{3}$ (C) $\frac{2}{4}$

   (B) $\frac{2}{3}$ (D) $\frac{3}{4}$

12 How many eighths are
equivalent to $\frac{2}{2}$?

$\frac{}{8}$

13 Which fraction is equivalent
to $\frac{2}{4}$?

Select **all** the correct answers.

   (A) $\frac{4}{2}$

   (B) $\frac{4}{8}$

   (C) $\frac{4}{6}$

   (D) $\frac{3}{6}$

   (E) $\frac{1}{2}$

1 Which is equivalent to 5?

Ⓐ $\frac{1}{5}$

Ⓑ $\frac{2}{3}$

Ⓒ $\frac{5}{3}$

Ⓓ $\frac{5}{1}$

2 Which is equivalent to $\frac{4}{4}$?

Ⓐ 4

Ⓑ 1

Ⓒ $\frac{4}{1}$

Ⓓ $\frac{1}{4}$

3 Which is equivalent to $\frac{24}{4}$?

Ⓐ 4

Ⓑ 6

Ⓒ 20

Ⓓ 24

4 What is the unknown number, n?

$\frac{6}{n} = 2$

$\frac{12}{4} = n$

5 Mara runs $\frac{8}{4}$ of a mile. How far does she run?

Ⓐ $\frac{32}{4}$ miles

Ⓑ 2 miles

Ⓒ 4 miles

Ⓓ $\frac{1}{2}$ mile

6 Oranges are shared during a soccer game. They are cut into slices as shown.

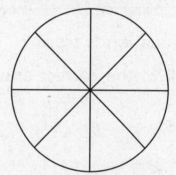

The soccer players eat a total of 48 orange slices.

How many whole oranges are eaten?

Ⓐ $\frac{1}{6}$

Ⓑ 6

Ⓒ 8

Ⓓ 12

Name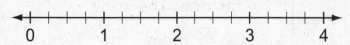

7 Plot a point to show $\frac{8}{4}$ on the number line.

```
◄──┼─┼─┼─┼─┼─┼─┼─┼─┼─┼─┼─┼─┼─┼─┼─┼──►
   0       1       2       3       4
```

8 Clark bought $\frac{4}{4}$ pounds of dog food. How many pounds of dog food did Clark buy?

Ⓐ 1

Ⓑ 2

Ⓒ 4

Ⓓ 8

9 Which equation is true?

Select **all** of the correct answers.

Ⓐ $\frac{5}{1} = \frac{1}{5}$

Ⓑ $\frac{24}{8} = 3$

Ⓒ $\frac{7}{7} = 7$

Ⓓ $\frac{18}{6} = 2$

Ⓔ $\frac{16}{4} = \frac{4}{1}$

10 What is the unknown number, *n*?

$n = \frac{2}{1}$

Ⓐ 8

Ⓑ 4

Ⓒ 2

Ⓓ 1

1 Shara uses $\frac{1}{3}$ cup of oil and $\frac{2}{3}$ cup of water in a recipe.

Which statement correctly compares the fractions?

(A) $\frac{1}{3} > \frac{2}{3}$ (C) $\frac{2}{3} > \frac{1}{3}$

(B) $\frac{1}{3} = \frac{2}{3}$ (D) $\frac{2}{3} < \frac{1}{3}$

2 Frank and Dwayne weed gardens that are the same size. Frank's garden is divided into 6 equal sections. Dwayne's garden is divided into 4 equal sections. Each boy has weeded 2 sections of his garden.

Fill in the correct symbol to compare the sections Frank and Dwayne weeded.

$\frac{2}{6} \bigcirc \frac{2}{4}$

3 Moira uses $\frac{3}{4}$ cup flour and $\frac{2}{4}$ cup sugar in a recipe.

Which statement correctly compares the fractions?

(A) $\frac{3}{4} > \frac{2}{4}$ (C) $\frac{2}{4} = \frac{3}{4}$

(B) $\frac{3}{4} < \frac{2}{4}$ (D) $\frac{2}{4} > \frac{3}{4}$

4 Eli, Beth, and Cory are reading the same book for class. Eli read $\frac{3}{4}$ of his book, Beth read $\frac{3}{8}$ of her book, and Cory read $\frac{3}{6}$ of his book.

Place an X in the table to show whether each comparison is correct.

	Yes	No
$\frac{3}{4} > \frac{3}{8}$		
$\frac{3}{6} < \frac{3}{8}$		
$\frac{3}{8} = \frac{3}{6}$		
$\frac{3}{6} < \frac{3}{4}$		

5 In a survey, $\frac{1}{3}$ of shoppers chose Friday as their favorite day to shop, and $\frac{1}{8}$ of shoppers chose Sunday.

Which statement correctly compares the fractions?

(A) $\frac{1}{3} = \frac{1}{8}$ (C) $\frac{1}{8} > \frac{1}{3}$

(B) $\frac{1}{3} < \frac{1}{8}$ (D) $\frac{1}{8} < \frac{1}{3}$

Name _____

6 In a survey, $\frac{1}{2}$ of students chose the swings as their favorite, and $\frac{1}{4}$ of students chose the monkey bars.

Which statement correctly compares the fractions?

Ⓐ $\frac{1}{4} > \frac{1}{2}$ Ⓒ $\frac{1}{2} < \frac{1}{4}$

Ⓑ $\frac{1}{4} < \frac{1}{2}$ Ⓓ $\frac{1}{2} = \frac{1}{4}$

7 Mark and Lisa are on the swim team. Mark swims $\frac{3}{8}$ mile each day. Lisa swims $\frac{5}{8}$ mile each day.

Select **all** the correct statements about the distances Mark and Lisa swam.

Ⓐ Mark swims farther than Lisa each day.

Ⓑ The distance Mark swims is less than Lisa each day.

Ⓒ Lisa swims the same distance as Mark each day.

Ⓓ Lisa swims farther than Mark each day.

Ⓔ The distance Lisa swims is less than Mark each day.

8 Ming uses $\frac{3}{4}$ cup of peanuts and $\frac{1}{4}$ cup of raisins to make a snack. Which statement correctly compares the fractions?

Ⓐ $\frac{3}{4} = \frac{1}{4}$ Ⓒ $\frac{3}{4} < \frac{1}{4}$

Ⓑ $\frac{1}{4} > \frac{3}{4}$ Ⓓ $\frac{3}{4} > \frac{1}{4}$

9 Alison used $\frac{7}{8}$ quart of orange juice and $\frac{3}{8}$ quart of cranberry juice to make some punch.

Place an X in the table to show if each comparison is true or false.

	True	False
$\frac{7}{8} < \frac{3}{8}$		
$\frac{7}{8} > \frac{3}{8}$		
$\frac{3}{8} < \frac{7}{8}$		
$\frac{3}{8} = \frac{7}{8}$		

10 In a survey, $\frac{1}{2}$ of the students chose summer as their favorite season, and $\frac{1}{8}$ chose winter. Which statement correctly compares the fractions?

Ⓐ $\frac{1}{2} = \frac{1}{8}$ Ⓒ $\frac{1}{8} < \frac{1}{2}$

Ⓑ $\frac{1}{2} < \frac{1}{8}$ Ⓓ $\frac{1}{8} > \frac{1}{2}$

1 Maria looked at her watch when it was time to leave for school.

What time did it show?

(A) 7:12 a.m.   (C) 8:12 a.m.

(B) 7:52 a.m.   (D) 8:52 a.m.

2 Luz left for the park at 2:27 p.m. She arrived at 3:09 p.m. How long in minutes did it take Luz to get to the park?

_____

3 Zane started painting a picture at 6:07 p.m. and finished at 6:42 p.m.

For how long did he paint his picture?

(A) 25 minutes

(B) 35 minutes

(C) 42 minutes

(D) 49 minutes

4 Chris left his house to walk his dog at 6:25 p.m. He returned home after 26 minutes. He talked to his neighbor outside for 10 minutes before going back inside.

Fill in the blanks with the correct answers.

Chris returned home at _____ p.m.

He went inside at _____ p.m.

5 Jasmine looks at a clock when she arrives at school.

At what time did Jasmine arrive?

(A) 3:08   (C) 8:05

(B) 3:41   (D) 8:17

6 Rory started playing a computer game at 3:15 p.m. and finished playing at 3:51 p.m.

For how long did Rory play the game?

(A) 35 minutes (C) 46 minutes

(B) 36 minutes (D) 66 minutes

Name _____

7 Terry wakes up for school at 5 minutes before 7 in the morning. At what time does Terry wake up?

Fill in the blanks with the numbers from the list to tell what time Terry wakes up.

Terry wakes up at

_____ : _____ a.m.

7	6	05	55

8 Clara looked at the clock on her way to band practice.

What time did it show?

Ⓐ 3:09 p.m.   Ⓒ 4:47 p.m.

Ⓑ 3:47 p.m.   Ⓓ 9:19 p.m.

9 A batch of muffins needs to bake in the oven for 22 minutes. They need to cool for at least 15 minutes before they can be eaten. Wade puts the muffins in the oven at 10:17 a.m.

Place an X in the table to show whether each statement is true or false.

	True	False
Wade can eat the muffins at 10:39 p.m.		
Wade can eat the muffins at 10:44 a.m.		
Wade takes the muffins out of the oven at 10:39 p.m.		
Wade takes the muffins out of the oven at 10:39 a.m.		

10 Omar started his homework at 4:20 p.m. and finished at 4:44 p.m.

For how long did he work on his homework?

Ⓐ 24 minutes   Ⓒ 44 minutes

Ⓑ 36 minutes   Ⓓ 64 minutes

1 Mrs. Baker fills a drum with 25 liters of water. Then she fills another drum with 19 liters of water.

What is the total liquid volume of water in both drums?

Ⓐ 6 liters   Ⓒ 44 liters

Ⓑ 34 liters   Ⓓ 46 liters

2 Select **all** the objects that have a mass less than 1 kilogram.

Ⓐ bed   Ⓓ eyeglasses

Ⓑ desk   Ⓔ plastic fork

Ⓒ eraser

3 Mrs. Bromley pours 26 liters of cold water and 17 liters of warm water into a barrel. How much water is in the barrel?

Ⓐ 9 liters   Ⓒ 41 liters

Ⓑ 33 liters   Ⓓ 43 liters

4 A barrel of water holds about 19 liters.

Place an X in the table to show whether each container will hold about 19 liters of water.

	Yes	No
bathtub		
large water bottle		
soup bowl		
large fish tank		
vase		

5 Mrs. Crocker fills a container with 17 liters of water. She then fills another container with 24 liters of water. What is the total liquid volume of water in both containers?

Ⓐ 7 liters   Ⓒ 37 liters

Ⓑ 31 liters   Ⓓ 41 liters

6 Abby fills a mug with tea. Which statement is true about the amount of tea?

Ⓐ The amount of tea is less than 1 milliliter.

Ⓑ The amount of tea is about 1 milliliter.

Ⓒ The amount of tea is more than 1 milliliter but less than 1 liter.

Ⓓ The amount of tea is more than 1 liter but less than 2 liters.

7 Select **all** the animals that would be best measured in kilograms.

Ⓐ bird

Ⓑ dog

Ⓒ goat

Ⓓ mouse

Ⓔ sheep

8 Which object weighs about 1 gram?

Ⓐ chair

Ⓑ paper clip

Ⓒ bag of flour

Ⓓ box of crayons

9 Alicia buys two packets of flower seeds. She buys a total of 75 grams of seeds. Which packets of seeds could Alicia have bought?

Select the **two** correct answers.

Ⓐ 25 grams

Ⓑ 30 grams

Ⓒ 35 grams

Ⓓ 45 grams

Ⓔ 75 grams

10 Markeya is prepping for a car wash. She fills a green tub with 28 liters of soapy water. She fills a red tub with 9 liters of water. How much more water is in the green tub than the red tub?

Ⓐ 19 liters

Ⓑ 21 liters

Ⓒ 28 liters

Ⓓ 29 liters

© Houghton Mifflin Harcourt Publishing Company

1 Amy's teacher made a bar graph to show the number of school lunches bought over a 5-day period by her class.

School Lunches Bought

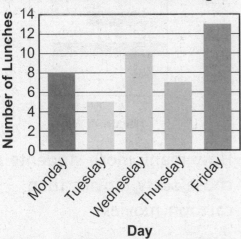

How many more lunches were bought on Friday than on Tuesday and Thursday combined?

Ⓐ 1

Ⓑ 6

Ⓒ 8

Ⓓ 13

2 Four types of sandwiches are offered at a class picnic. The table shows the number of sandwiches chosen.

Class Picnic Sandwiches

Sandwich	Number of Sandwiches
Cheese	8
Ham	10
Tuna	4
Chicken	14

Draw the bars to represent these data in the bar graph.

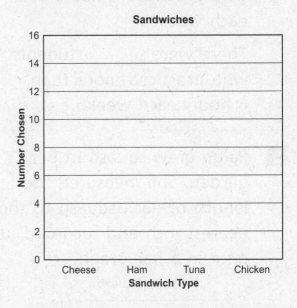

3 Jae made a picture graph to show the number of students who play baseball after school. This is the key to his picture graph.

Key: Each ⚲ = 2 students.

How does Jae represent 9 students?

Ⓐ ⚲⚲⚲⚲   Ⓑ ⚲⚲⚲⚲⚲⚲   Ⓒ ⚲⚲⚲⚲⚲   Ⓓ ⚲⚲⚲⚲⚲⚲⚲⚲⚲⚲

4 Yuji made a bar graph to show the numbers of hours each student in his music class practiced each week.

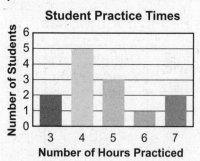

Student Practice Times

Number of Students / Number of Hours Practiced

Complete the statements to describe the graph.

There were _____ students who practiced 4 hours or less each week.

There were _____ students who practiced more than 6 hours each week.

5 Paige grew squash in her garden. She measured the length of each squash to the nearest inch and recorded her data in a bar graph.

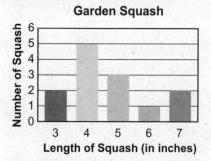

Garden Squash

Number of Squash / Length of Squash (in inches)

How many more squash were 4 inches long than were 7 inches long? _____

6 Lucy made a bar graph to show her classmates' favorite types of movies.

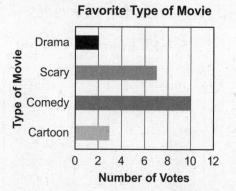

Favorite Type of Movie

Type of Movie / Number of Votes

How many more students chose scary movies than cartoon movies?

(A) 3   (C) 7

(B) 4   (D) 10

7 The principal made a bar graph to show the number of absent students at a school over a five-day period.

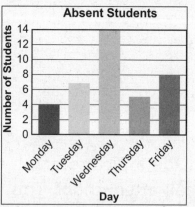

Absent Students

Number of Students / Day

On which day were twice as many students absent as on Tuesday?

(A) Monday   (C) Thursday

(B) Wednesday   (D) Friday

1 What is the length of the nail to the nearest fourth-inch?

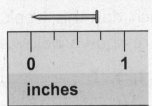

0   1
inches

Ⓐ $\frac{1}{4}$ inch   Ⓒ $\frac{3}{4}$ inch

Ⓑ $\frac{1}{2}$ inch   Ⓓ 1 inch

2 Kayla measured objects with an inch ruler. Each was about 1 inch wide. Which objects could she have measured?

Select the **two** correct answers.

Ⓐ
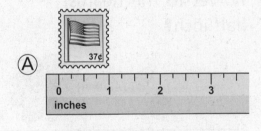

Ⓑ
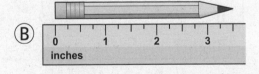

Ⓒ
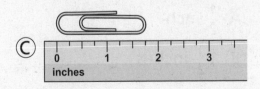

Ⓓ
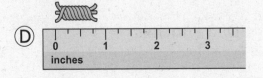

3 What is the length of the leaf to the nearest half-inch?

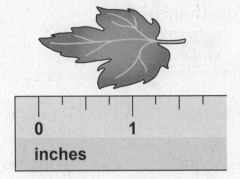

0   1
inches

Ⓐ $\frac{1}{2}$ inch   Ⓒ $1\frac{1}{2}$ inches

Ⓑ 1 inch   Ⓓ 2 inches

4 Mr. Barton measures the screws on his workbench. He records the measurements and the number of each screw in a table.

Length (in inches)	Number of Screws
$\frac{1}{2}$	1
1	2
$1\frac{1}{2}$	2
$2\frac{1}{2}$	1

To show the data on the line plot, how many Xs should Mr. Barton draw above the $1\frac{1}{2}$ mark?

5 What is the length of the ribbon to the nearest fourth-inch?

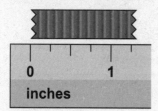

Ⓐ $\frac{1}{4}$ inch   Ⓒ $1\frac{1}{4}$ inches

Ⓑ 1 inch   Ⓓ $1\frac{1}{2}$ inches

---

6 June made a line plot to show the number of hours each player on her basketball team practiced every week.

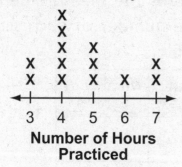

Number of Hours Practiced

Two more players joined the team, and each of those players practiced 7 hours a week. What should June add to the line plot to show these new data?

Ⓐ Add 1 more X above 3 and 1 more X above 4.

Ⓑ Add 1 more X above 7.

Ⓒ Add 2 more Xs above 6.

Ⓓ Add 2 more Xs above 7.

7 Jeremy recorded the number of pages he wrote in his journal each day this week. His data are shown below.

2, 3, 1, 2, 1, 5, 1

Draw Xs on the line plot to represent the number of pages Jeremy wrote each day.

Journal Pages

Number of Pages Written Each Day

---

8 What is the length of the flower to the nearest half-inch?

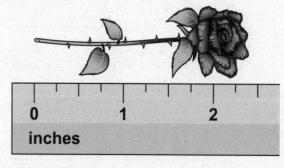

Ⓐ $\frac{1}{2}$ inch

Ⓑ $1\frac{1}{2}$ inches

Ⓒ 2 inches

Ⓓ $2\frac{1}{2}$ inches

46

1 A square has a side length of 1 unit. What is the area of the square?

Ⓐ 1 unit   Ⓒ 1 square unit

Ⓑ 4 units   Ⓓ 4 square units

2 Which of these figures have a shaded area equal to 16 square units?

Select **all** the correct answers.

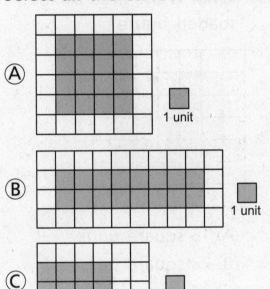

3 Each square has an area of 1 square unit.

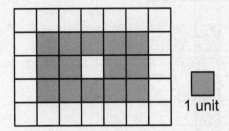

1 unit

What is a correct way to find the area of the shaded figure?

Select **all** the correct answers.

Ⓐ Count all the shaded squares.

Ⓑ Count the numbers of sides around the figure.

Ⓒ Add the number of square units for each row: 5 + 4 + 5.

Ⓓ Add the number of square units for each row: 5 + 5 + 5.

Ⓔ Add the number of square units for each row and subtract 1 square unit: 5 + 5 + 5 − 1.

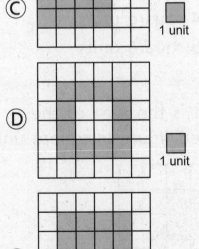
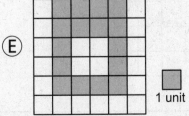

4 What is the area of the shaded figure?

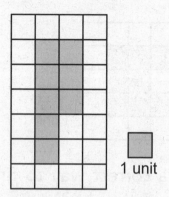

1 unit

(A) 1 square unit

(B) 6 square units

(C) 8 square units

(D) 20 square units

5 Ace is planning where to place a feed box on his farm for his horse.

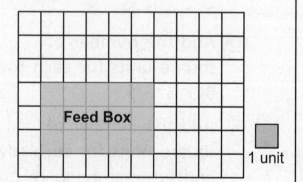

Feed Box

1 unit

What is the area of the feed box?

(A) 5 square units

(B) 10 square units

(C) 12 square units

(D) 15 square units

6 What is the area of the shaded figure in square units?

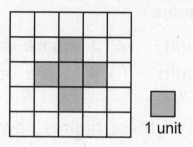

1 unit

7 What is the area of the shaded figure?

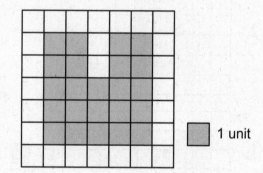

1 unit

(A) 15 square units

(B) 23 square units

(C) 24 square units

(D) 25 square units

8 What is the area of the shaded figure in square units?

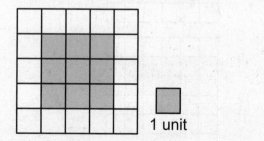

1 unit

1 In the figure, each unit square measures 1 square foot.

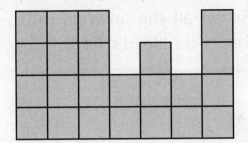

What is the area of the figure in square feet?

_____

2 Rosa's bedroom door is 4 feet wide and 6 feet tall. She puts up a poster on the door. The poster is 2 feet wide and 3 feet long.

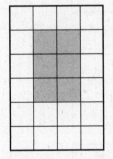

How many square feet of her door are not covered by the poster?

Ⓐ 5

Ⓑ 6

Ⓒ 18

Ⓓ 24

3 A figure and a unit square with an area of 1 square foot are shown.

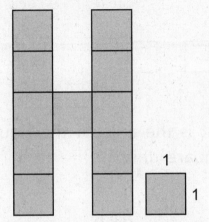

What is the area of the shape?

Ⓐ 3 square feet

Ⓑ 10 square feet

Ⓒ 11 square feet

Ⓓ 15 square feet

4 A class makes art tiles that measure 1 square foot each. A rectangular display of the tiles is shown.

Each student makes 1 tile. How many students are in the class?

Ⓐ 3   Ⓒ 12

Ⓑ 6   Ⓓ 27

5 A figure is shown next to a unit square that measures 1 unit on each side.

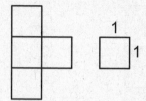

What is the area of the figure in square units?

Ⓐ 3 Ⓒ 5
Ⓑ 4 Ⓓ 6

6 Ben's workroom has an area of 144 square feet. He has a table, a counter, and a desk to use as a work surface.

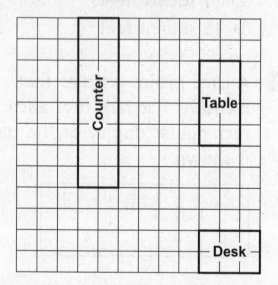

What is the total area in square feet of the work surface he can use?

Ⓐ 24 Ⓒ 114
Ⓑ 30 Ⓓ 144

7 The area of Lloyd's floor is 36 square feet.

Select **all** the answers that could be Lloyd's floor.

Ⓐ

Ⓑ
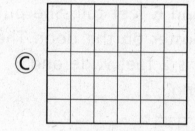

Ⓒ

Ⓓ
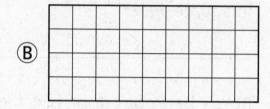

Ⓔ
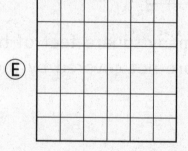

1 A figure is made up of unit squares. Each unit square is 1 square centimeter.

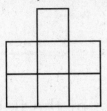

What is the area of the figure in square centimeters?

Ⓐ 6   Ⓒ 8
Ⓑ 7   Ⓓ 9

2 Each unit square in the figure is 1 square meter, as shown.

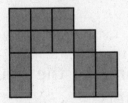

What is the area of the figure in square meters?

3 A figure is made up of unit squares. Each unit square is 1 square meter.

What is the area of the figure in square meters?

Ⓐ 9   Ⓒ 4
Ⓑ 5   Ⓓ 1

4 Each unit square in the figure is 1 square foot, as shown.

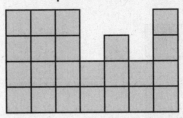

What is the area of the figure in square feet?

5 A figure is made up of unit squares, as shown. Each unit square is 1 square inch.

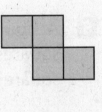

What is the area of the figure in square inches?

Ⓐ 1   Ⓒ 4
Ⓑ 2   Ⓓ 6

6 A figure is made up of unit squares, as shown. Each unit square is 1 square foot.

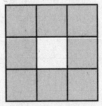

What is the area of the figure in square feet?

Ⓐ 1   Ⓒ 6
Ⓑ 3   Ⓓ 8

Name _____

7 Each unit square in the figure is 1 square inch, as shown.

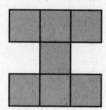

What is the area of the figure in square inches?

_____

8 A figure is made up of unit squares, as shown. Each unit square is 1 square centimeter.

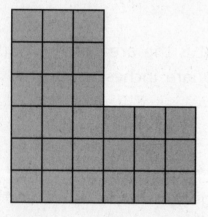

What is the area of the figure in square centimeters?

Ⓐ 36
Ⓑ 27
Ⓒ 18
Ⓓ 9

9 Each unit square in the figure is 1 square meter, as shown.

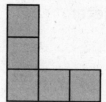

What is the area of the figure in square meters?

_____

10 A figure is made up of unit squares, as shown. Each unit square is 1 square meter.

What is the area of the figure in square meters?

Ⓐ 2
Ⓑ 3
Ⓒ 5
Ⓓ 6

1 The drawing shows the kitchen in Ben's school. Each unit square is 1 square yard.

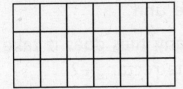

Which equation can Ben use to find the area of the kitchen?

(A) 3 + 6 = 9

(B) 6 ÷ 3 = 2

(C) 3 × 6 = 18

(D) 3 × 5 + 6 × 1 = 21

---

2 Brady is placing square tiles on the kitchen floor. Each tile is 1 square foot.

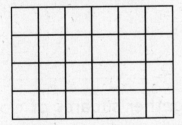

Which of these expressions can Brady use to find the area?

Select **all** of the correct answers.

(A) 4 × 6

(B) 4 + 4 + 4 + 4

(C) 4 × 5 + 6 × 1

(D) 4 + 6 + 4 + 6

(E) 6 + 6 + 6 + 6

3 The drawing shows Erik's plan for a dog run. Each unit square is 1 square meter.

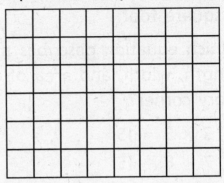

Which equation can Erik use to find the area of the dog run?

(A) 6 + 8 = 14

(B) 6 × 8 = 48

(C) 6 × 2 + 8 × 2 = 28

(D) 6 × 6 + 8 × 2 = 52

---

4 Simon draws a sketch of a toy box on grid paper. Each unit square is 1 square inch.

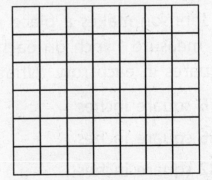

What equation can help him find the area of the toy box in square inches?

_____ × _____ = _____

5 The story corner in a library is a rectangle covered in 15 carpet tiles. Each carpet tile is 1 square foot.

Which equation describes the length, width, and area of the story corner?

Ⓐ $3 \times 5 = 15$
Ⓑ $7 + 8 = 15$
Ⓒ $3 + 5 + 3 + 5 = 16$
Ⓓ $2 \times 3 + 4 \times 3 = 18$

6 A rectangle that is 2 units wide and 7 units long is covered in tiles that measure 1 square unit.

How many tiles does it take to cover the rectangle?

Ⓐ 9
Ⓑ 10
Ⓒ 14
Ⓓ 18

7 A rectangle is 3 units wide and is covered by 18 unit tiles. Shade the model to represent the rectangle.

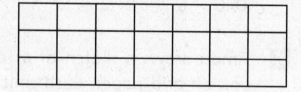

8 Ms. Johnson makes a place mat by sewing together squares of cloth that measure 1 inch on each side. She uses 8 rows of squares with 8 squares in each row. What is the area of the place mat?

Ⓐ 16 square inches
Ⓑ 56 square inches
Ⓒ 32 square inches
Ⓓ 64 square inches

1 Elizabeth has a rectangular garden in her yard. The garden has a length of 8 feet and a width of 6 feet.

What is the area of the garden?

The area of the garden is _____ square feet.

2 A carpenter makes a table that is 5 feet wide and 6 feet long. She wants the table to have an area of 40 square feet. How much longer should the carpenter make the table?

Ⓐ 2 feet

Ⓑ 4 feet

Ⓒ 10 feet

Ⓓ 8 feet

3 There are two dog runs at the animal clinic. The first dog run is shown below.

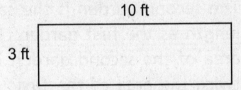

10 ft

3 ft

The second dog run is the same length as the first dog run. The area of the second dog run is twice the area of the first dog run.

What is the width in feet of the second dog run?

Ⓐ 2   Ⓒ 6

Ⓑ 3   Ⓓ 12

4 There are two sandboxes in the play area. The first sandbox is 5 feet long and 4 feet wide. The second sandbox is the same length as the first sandbox. The area of the second sandbox is twice the area of the first sandbox.

What is the width of the second sandbox?

Ⓐ 2 feet   Ⓒ 8 feet

Ⓑ 4 feet   Ⓓ 10 feet

5 Mrs. Parker has two gardens in her yard. The first garden is 6 feet long and 4 feet wide. The second garden is the same length as the first garden. The area of the second garden is twice the area of the first garden.

What is the width in feet of the second garden?

(A) 2   (C) 6

(B) 3   (D) 8

6 Lydia is knitting a blanket. The blanket will be 5 feet long and 4 feet wide.

What will the area in square feet of the blanket be?

(A) 24   (C) 15

(B) 20   (D) 9

7 Raul makes a rectangular sign for the school fair. It has a length of 9 inches and a width of 8 inches. What is the area of the sign?

The area of the sign is _____ square inches.

8 What is the area of the rectangle in square centimeters?

3 cm

7 cm

(A) 10   (C) 20

(B) 13   (D) 21

9 Etta prints a photograph that is 7 inches long and 5 inches wide. What is the area of the photograph?

The area of the photograph is _____ square inches.

10 The rectangle has an area of 12 square meters.

2 m

What is the length of the rectangle in meters?

(A) 6   (C) 14

(B) 10   (D) 24

1 The shallow end of the pool is 3 meters wide and 2 meters long. The deep end of the pool is 3 meters wide and 7 meters long.

Which equation shows how to find the total area of the pool in square meters?

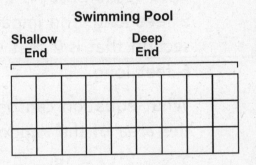

Swimming Pool

Shallow End   Deep End

(A) $2 \times 7 + 3 \times 3 = 23$

(B) $3 \times 2 + 3 \times 7 = 27$

(C) $9 \times 2 + 9 \times 7 = 27$

(D) $3 \times 2 + 2 \times 2 + 3 \times 2 + 7 \times 2 = 27$

2 In a yearbook, two student clubs share a page. The areas taken by the chess club and the birdwatching club are shown. Each square represents 1 square inch.

Which equations describe the total area of the page in square inches?

Select **all** the correct equations.

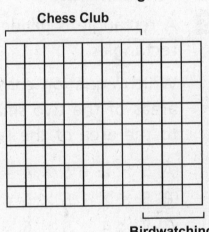

Yearbook Page

Chess Club

Birdwatching Club

(A) $3 \times 8 = 24$

(B) $7 \times 8 = 56$

(C) $8 \times 10 = 80$

(D) $8 \times (3 + 7) = 80$

(E) $7 \times 8 + 3 \times 8 = 80$

3 A large rectangle is divided into 2 sections. One section has an area of 4×6 square units and a smaller section has an area of 4×3 square units. Which equation can be used to find the total area in square units?

(A) $3 \times 6 + 3 \times 2 = 24$

(B) $4 \times 3 + 3 \times 6 = 30$

(C) $4 \times 4 = 16$

(D) $9 \times 4 = 36$

4 Maria's window box is planted with peas and impatiens. The peas take up a section that is 2 feet wide and 2 feet long. The impatiens are in a section that is 2 feet wide and 6 feet long.

What equation can be used to find the area of the window box?

$2 \times$ _____ $= 16$

Window Box

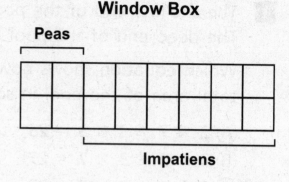

5 A rectangle is divided into two smaller rectangles.

Which equation correctly shows how the areas of the two smaller rectangles add up to the area of the large rectangle?

Ⓐ $5 \times 2 + 5 \times 4 = 5 \times 6$

Ⓑ $5 \times 2 + 6 \times 5 = 5 \times 4$

Ⓒ $5 \times 4 + 5 \times 6 = 5 \times 2$

Ⓓ $10 \times 5 + 20 \times 5 = 30 \times 5$

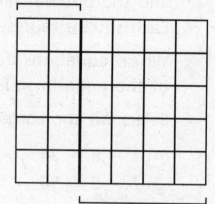

Rectangle 1

Rectangle 2

6 A rectangle is divided into 24 unit squares.

Which equation shows how it could be divided into two smaller rectangles with the same total area?

Ⓐ $4 \times 6 = 2 \times 3 + 2 \times 9$

Ⓑ $4 \times 6 = 2 \times 4 + 4 \times 4$

Ⓒ $4 \times 6 = 3 \times 4 + 6 \times 2$

Ⓓ $4 \times 6 = 8 \times 2 + 8 \times 1$

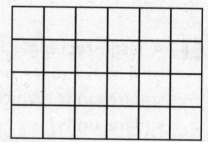

1 What is the area in square inches of the figure shown?

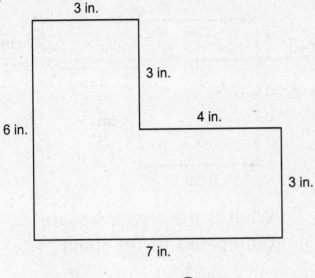

3 in.

3 in.

4 in.

6 in.

3 in.

7 in.

Ⓐ 26   Ⓒ 39

Ⓑ 30   Ⓓ 42

2 Mrs. Rios puts tape around the section of wall shown below to indicate the area of the mural she will paint.

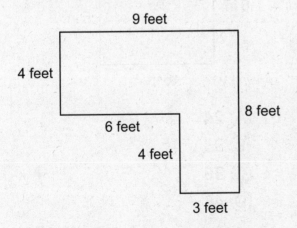

9 feet

4 feet

6 feet

8 feet

4 feet

3 feet

What is the area in square feet of the mural she wants to paint?

_____

3 What is the area in square meters of the figure shown?

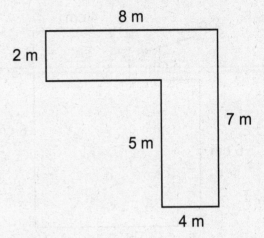

8 m

2 m

7 m

5 m

4 m

Ⓐ 26

Ⓑ 36

Ⓒ 44

Ⓓ 56

4 What is the area in square inches of the figure shown?

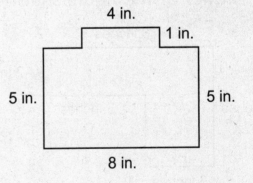

4 in.

1 in.

5 in.

5 in.

8 in.

_____

Name _____

5 What is the area in square centimeters of the figure shown?

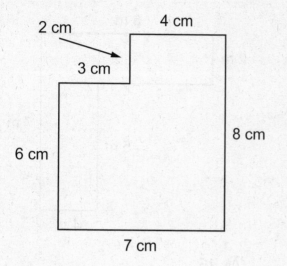

2 cm

4 cm

3 cm

8 cm

6 cm

7 cm

Ⓐ 30
Ⓑ 50
Ⓒ 56
Ⓓ 74

6 What is the area in square inches of the figure shown?

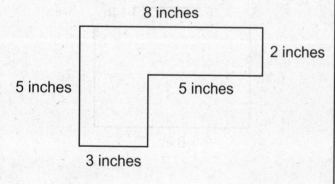

8 inches

2 inches

5 inches

5 inches

3 inches

Ⓐ 25
Ⓑ 26
Ⓒ 31
Ⓓ 40

7 Kendra used markers to color the shape shown below.

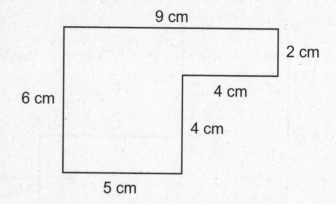

9 cm

2 cm

6 cm

4 cm

4 cm

5 cm

What is the area in square centimeters of the shape?

_____

8 What is the area in square inches of the figure shown?

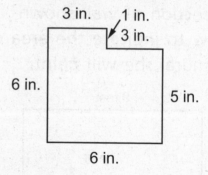

3 in.

1 in.

3 in.

6 in.

5 in.

6 in.

Ⓐ 24
Ⓑ 33
Ⓒ 36
Ⓓ 48

1 Tia wants to put a piece of blue yarn around a picture she drew.

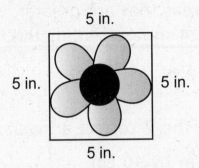

5 in.

5 in.   5 in.

5 in.

How many inches of blue yarn does she need for the perimeter of the picture?

Ⓐ 5   Ⓒ 20

Ⓑ 10   Ⓓ 25

2 Mr. Howard puts wood trim around his window.

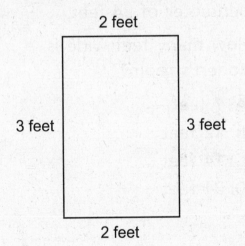

2 feet

3 feet   3 feet

2 feet

How many feet of wood trim does he need for the perimeter of the window?

_____

3 Doug draws a model of his family garden. It is a perfect square.

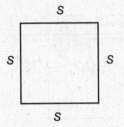

s

s   s

s

The perimeter of the garden is 20 feet. What is the length of each side of the garden in feet?

Ⓐ 4   Ⓒ 16

Ⓑ 5   Ⓓ 25

4 Kendra made a window decoration in the shape shown.

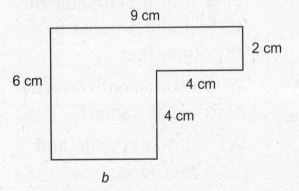

9 cm

2 cm

6 cm   4 cm

4 cm

b

She glued ribbon around the edges and used 30 cm of ribbon. What is the unknown side length, b, in cm?

_____

Name

5 Gina drew a picture with the measurements shown.

8 in.

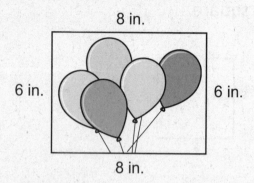

6 in.   6 in.

8 in.

She wants to put tape around the edges. What length of tape in inches will she use?

Ⓐ 14

Ⓑ 28

Ⓒ 48

Ⓓ 49

6 Verna's family has a bicycle shed with a perimeter of 18 feet and an area of 18 square feet.

Which statement correctly describes the shed?

Ⓐ It is 1 foot wide and 8 feet long.

Ⓑ It is 2 feet wide and 7 feet long.

Ⓒ It is 3 feet wide and 6 feet long.

Ⓓ It is 4 feet wide and 5 feet long.

7 For a quilting project, Bekka wants rectangles of fabric with perimeters of 24 centimeters but areas that are greater than 24 square centimeters.

What size rectangles can she use?

Select the **2** correct answers.

Ⓐ 2 cm by 10 cm

Ⓑ 3 cm by 4 cm

Ⓒ 4 cm by 8 cm

Ⓓ 5 cm by 7 cm

Ⓔ 6 cm by 6 cm

Ⓕ 7 cm by 6 cm

8 Robert's room is a rectangle that is 10 feet long. It has a perimeter of 34 feet.

How many feet wide is Robert's room?

Ⓐ 7 feet

Ⓑ 12 feet

Ⓒ 14 feet

Ⓓ 24 feet

1 Which quadrilateral has opposite sides that are the same length, but not all the sides are the same length?

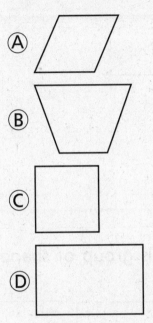

Ⓐ

Ⓑ

Ⓒ

Ⓓ

2 Which quadrilateral(s) **always** has 4 right angles?

Select **all** the correct answers.

Ⓐ square
Ⓑ rhombus
Ⓒ rectangle
Ⓓ trapezoid
Ⓔ parallelogram

3 Which quadrilateral has four sides that appear to be the same length and four right angles?

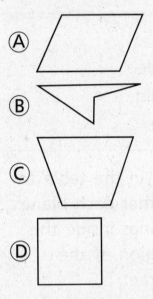

Ⓐ

Ⓑ

Ⓒ

Ⓓ

4 Which quadrilateral has sides that are all different lengths?

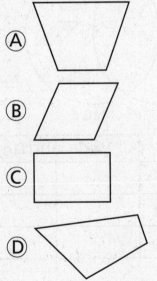

Ⓐ

Ⓑ

Ⓒ

Ⓓ

5 Which word BEST describes this shape?

(A) square

(B) rectangle

(C) trapezoid

(D) triangle

6 Place an X in the table to show whether each plane shape belongs inside the overlap region of the Venn diagram.

Polygons with Right Angles   **Quadrilaterals**

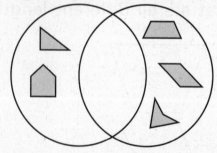

	Yes	No
Square		
Pentagon		
Rectangle		

7 How many more right angles does a rectangle have than this triangle?

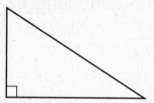

(A) 4

(B) 3

(C) 2

(D) 1

8 Look at this group of shapes.

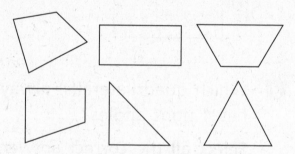

If the shapes were sorted by number of sides, how many groups could be made?

_____ groups

1 Which circle has $\frac{1}{3}$ of its area shaded in?

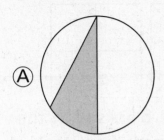
Ⓐ

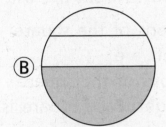
Ⓑ

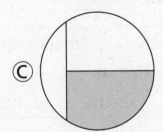
Ⓒ

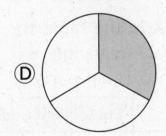
Ⓓ

2 What fraction of the shape is shaded?

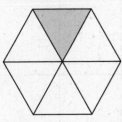

$\frac{1}{\boxed{}}$

3 The square has been divided into halves.

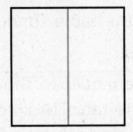

What line added to the square would divide it into fourths?

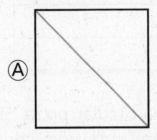
Ⓐ

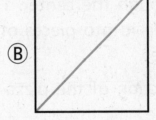
Ⓑ

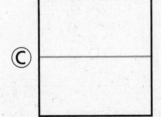
Ⓒ

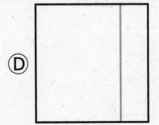
Ⓓ

4 Nick plans to divide his work table into thirds. He wants to use $\frac{1}{3}$ of the table to work on birdhouses.

Shade the model to show the part of the table Nick could use for building birdhouses.

5 Nina has a circular pizza. She makes three cuts from edge to edge through the center. The cuts divide it into pieces of equal sizes.

What fraction of the pizza is each piece?

Ⓐ $\frac{1}{3}$ Ⓒ $\frac{1}{6}$

Ⓑ $\frac{1}{4}$ Ⓓ $\frac{1}{8}$

6 What fractional part of the triangle is shaded?

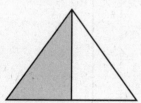

Ⓐ $\frac{1}{2}$ Ⓒ $\frac{1}{4}$

Ⓑ $\frac{1}{3}$ Ⓓ $\frac{1}{6}$

7 Reva divides two identical squares as shown.

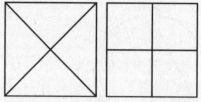

Fill in the blanks with the correct words from the list.

The sections of the square on the left are _____ the sections of the square on the right. Each square is divided into _____ .

larger than	smaller than
the same size as	
halves fourths eighths	

8 Place an X in the table to show if each rectangle is divided into equal parts.

	Equal	Not Equal

Practice Test

Item	Content Focus	DOK	Record
1	Fluently multiply and divide within 100.	1	
2	Understand a fraction $\frac{a}{b}$ as the quantity formed by a parts of size $\frac{1}{b}$. Partition shapes into parts with equal areas.	2	
3	Determine the unknown number in a multiplication or division equation.	1	
4	Solve problems involving addition and subtraction of time in minutes.	2	
5	Solve two-step word problems using the four operations.	2	
6	Fluently add and subtract within 1000.	1	
7	Use multiplication and division within 100 to solve word problems.	2	
8	Draw and use a scaled picture graph and a scaled bar graph.	2	
9	Explain equivalence of fractions and compare fractions.	3	
10	Understand division as an unknown-factor problem.	2	
11	Identify and explain arithmetic patterns.	3	
12	Solve problems involving perimeters of polygons.	2	
13	Interpret whole-number quotients of whole numbers.	2	
14	Understand concepts of area measurement. Measure areas by counting unit squares. Relate area to the operations of multiplication and addition.	3	
15	Round whole numbers to the nearest 10 or 100.	1	
16	Explain equivalence of fractions and compare fractions.	3	
17	Draw and use a scaled picture graph and a scaled bar graph.	2	
18	Use multiplication and division within 100 to solve word problems.	2	
19	Multiply one-digit whole numbers by multiples of 10 in the range 10–90.	1	
20	Understand that shapes in different categories may share attributes.	2	
21	Apply properties of operations as strategies to multiply and divide.	2	
22	Solve problems involving perimeters of polygons.	2	
23	Identify and explain arithmetic patterns.	3	
24	Solve one-step word problems involving masses or volumes.	2	
25	Understand a fraction $\frac{a}{b}$ as the quantity formed by a parts of size $\frac{1}{b}$. Partition shapes into parts with equal areas.	2	
26	Interpret products of whole numbers.	1	

Name _____

Item	Content Focus	DOK	Record
27	Explain equivalence of fractions and compare fractions.	3	
28	Fluently multiply and divide within 100.	1	
29	Understand concepts of area measurement. Measure areas by counting unit squares. Relate area to the operations of multiplication and addition.	2	
30	Solve one-step word problems involving masses or volumes.	2	
31	Represent fractions on a number line diagram.	2	
32	Record on a line plot lengths measured in halves or fourths of an inch.	2	
33	Solve two-step word problems using the four operations.	2	
34	Use multiplication and division within 100 to solve word problems.	3	
35	Solve two-step word problems using the four operations.	3	
36	Recognize area as additive.	3	

1 Fill in the blanks with the correct answers from the list.

$4 \times 6 =$ _____

_____ $\div$ _____ $= 4$

| 24 | 4 | 6 |

2 Chun and Jake plant a garden. They separate the garden into four equal parts. Three parts will be used to grow corn, and the rest will be used for beans. Which part of the garden will be used for growing beans?

Ⓐ $\frac{1}{8}$ Ⓒ 3

Ⓑ $\frac{1}{4}$ Ⓓ 4

3 Which of these is the unknown number in the equation?

$7 \times \boxed{} = 21$

Ⓐ 2   Ⓒ 14

Ⓑ 3   Ⓓ 17

4 Natalie's class has lunch, art, math, and reading on Tuesday afternoons. The start and end time of each activity is shown in the table.

Activity	Start Time	End Time
Lunch	12:00 p.m.	12:25 p.m.
Art	12:45 p.m.	1:20 p.m.
Math	1:20 p.m.	1:45 p.m.
Reading	2:00 p.m.	2:30 p.m.

Which activity takes the most time?

Ⓐ lunch   Ⓒ math

Ⓑ art   Ⓓ reading

5 Tamara has 5 packs of cards that have 5 cards each. She gives some cards to Ali. Tamara has 19 cards now. How many cards does she give to Ali?

Ⓐ 25   Ⓒ 13

Ⓑ 19   Ⓓ 6

6 Solve.

625 + 110 =

Ⓐ 120   Ⓒ 735

Ⓑ 515   Ⓓ 800

7 Charissa has a rock collection. She has 64 rocks in all. She puts an equal number of rocks into 8 bags. How many rocks are in each bag?

Write an expression to solve the problem. Then write the number of rocks in each bag.

_____

There are _____ rocks in each bag.

8 Ms. Nguyen's class voted on their favorite sports. Six students voted for baseball. Three more students voted for swimming than for baseball. Basketball had one more vote than swimming. Five fewer students voted for soccer than for swimming.

Write the letter of each sport below the correct bar on the chart to show how many students voted for each sport.

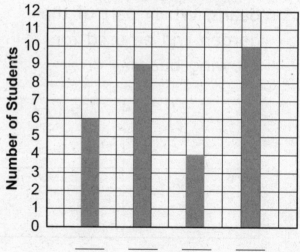

Favorite Sports of Ms. Nguyen's Class

A. Baseball   C. Swimming

B. Soccer   D. Basketball

9 Select **all** the choices that are equivalent to the fraction indicated on the number line.

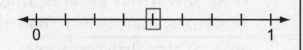

(A)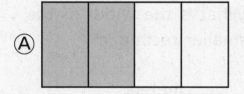

(B) $\frac{3}{4}$

(C) $\frac{1}{2}$

(D)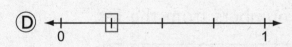

(E) $\frac{4}{1}$

(F) $\frac{2}{2}$

10 Which of the following numbers can be used to complete the equations below?

$5 \times \boxed{} = \boxed{}$

$45 \div 5 = \boxed{}$

(A) 5, 9   (C) 5, 40

(B) 9, 6   (D) 9, 45

11 The pattern shown was created by adding the same amount each time to get the next number.

15, 35, 55, 75, ...

What will be the seventh number in the pattern?

_____

12 Jonah builds a rectangular pen for his goats. The length of the pen is 5 meters and the area of the pen is 20 square meters.

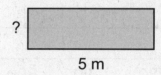

5 m

Jonah doubles the area of the original pen. The length of the new pen stays the same. What is the width of the new pen?

(A) 4 meters   (C) 10 meters

(B) 8 meters   (D) 40 meters

13 Reese has 28 apples. How can she put the apples into bags so there are none left over?

Ⓐ 2 bags of 8 apples

Ⓑ 3 bags of 10 apples

Ⓒ 4 bags of 7 apples

Ⓓ 9 bags of 3 apples

14 A rectangle is 7 meters long and 5 meters wide. A second rectangle is also 7 meters long, but it has an area that is 14 square meters less than the area of the first rectangle. What is the width of the smaller rectangle?

_____ meters

15 What is 788 rounded to the nearest 10 and to the nearest 100?

Fill in the boxes with the correct numbers from the list.

Rounded to the Nearest Ten	Rounded to the Nearest Hundred

| 700 | 780 | 790 | 800 | 810 |

16 Which statement is true?

Ⓐ $\frac{2}{4} < \frac{2}{6}$ because the numerators are the same, and $4 < 6$.

Ⓑ $\frac{2}{4} > \frac{2}{8}$ because $\frac{2}{4}$ represents a larger part of a whole than $\frac{2}{8}$.

Ⓒ $\frac{4}{8} = \frac{4}{4}$ because each fraction represents an equal number of pieces.

Ⓓ $\frac{1}{6} > \frac{3}{6}$ because the denominators are the same, but 1 is less than 3.

17 Hakeem asked all the students in his class about the kinds of pets they have. Some of the results are shown in the table. The number of students that have dogs is 4 less than the number that have cats. The number of students that have fish is 8 less than the number that have dogs.

Write the missing numbers in the table.

Type of Pet	Number of Students
Cat	16
Dog	
Fish	
Other	5

Complete the bar graph to represent the data correctly.

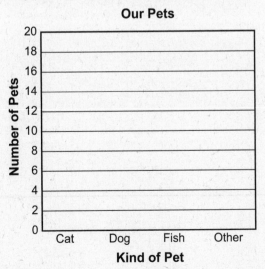

18 Mario has 56 erasers. He makes packs with 8 erasers in each pack. How many packs can Mario make if he uses all the erasers?

Write an equation to solve the problem. Then write the correct answer on the second line.

_____

_____ packs of erasers

19 Maya wrote the expression 3 × 40 on the board.

Select **all** of the expressions that are equal to Maya's expression.

Ⓐ 6 × 20

Ⓑ 1 × 12

Ⓒ 60 × 4

Ⓓ 4 × 30

Ⓔ 10 × 3

20 Write the letter of each polygon in the correct place in the table.

Quadrilaterals with 4 Right Angles	Quadrilaterals with No Right Angles	Not a Quadrilateral

A

B

C

D

E

F

21 Consider the expression 6×7.

Part A

Which of these expressions is equal to 6×7?

(A) $(3 \times 7) + (3 \times 7)$

(B) $(2 + 7) \times (3 + 7)$

(C) $(2 \times 7) + (5 \times 7)$

(D) $(6 \times 4) + (6 \times 2)$

Part B

What is the value of 6×7?

_____

© Houghton Mifflin Harcourt Publishing Company

22 Han is designing a garden for his yard. He draws a sketch of his garden.

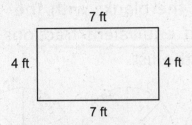

7 ft

4 ft   4 ft

7 ft

Select **all** of the polygons with the same perimeter as Han's garden.

Ⓐ
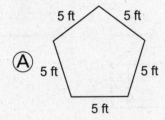
5 ft 5 ft
5 ft 5 ft
5 ft

Ⓑ
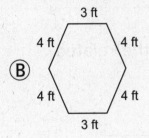
3 ft
4 ft 4 ft
4 ft 4 ft
3 ft

Ⓒ
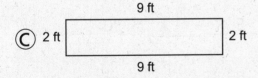
9 ft
2 ft   2 ft
9 ft

Ⓓ
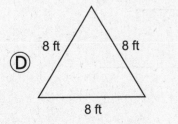
8 ft 8 ft
8 ft

Ⓔ
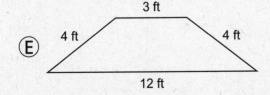
3 ft
4 ft   4 ft
12 ft

23 Fill in the blanks with the correct answers from the list. Each answer can be used more than once.

The sum of two odd numbers will be _____.

The sum of an even number and an odd number will be _____.

The sum of two even numbers will be _____.

even	odd

24 Matthew has 6 buckets of water. Each bucket has 8 liters of water in it. How much water does Matthew have?

Fill in the blanks with the correct answers from the list to complete the equation and solve the problem.

___ ___ ___ = ___

____ liters

×	÷	6	8	48	42	w

25 Shade the model to show $\frac{1}{2}$.

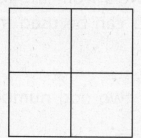

26 Liza has 6 boxes of colored pencils. Each box has 8 pencils in it.

Select **all** of the expressions that show how many colored pencils there are in all.

Ⓐ 6 + 8

Ⓑ 6 × 8

Ⓒ 8 + 6

Ⓓ 8 × 6

Ⓔ 8 + 8 + 8 + 8 + 8 + 8

Ⓕ 6 + 6 + 6 + 6 + 6 + 6

27 Liam drew the fraction models shown.

Fill in the blanks with the correct equivalent fractions from the list.

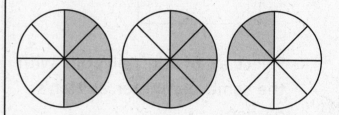

_____   _____   _____

$\frac{3}{4}$	$\frac{1}{2}$	$\frac{1}{4}$

28 Complete the related equations.

6 × 5 = _____

5 × _____ = 30

30 ÷ _____ = 6

30 ÷ 6 = _____

29 Rachel's back porch is shown.

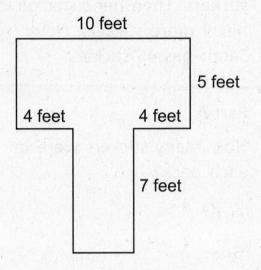

10 feet

5 feet

4 feet   4 feet

7 feet

What is the area of the porch in square feet?

Ⓐ 14 square feet

Ⓑ 26 square feet

Ⓒ 50 square feet

Ⓓ 64 square feet

30 Lisa and Joshua had containers filled with different amounts of water measured in milliliters.

Write the correct numbers from the list to show the amount of liquid in milliliters in each container.

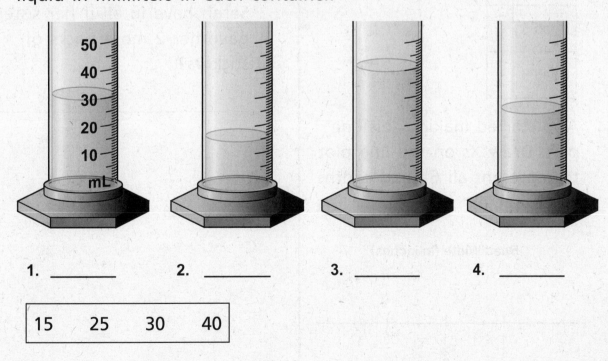

50
40
30
20
10
mL

1. _____   2. _____   3. _____   4. _____

| 15 | 25 | 30 | 40 |

31 Plot a point at $\frac{5}{4}$ on the number line.

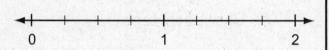

32 Alya measured the size of several beads. The widths are shown in the table.

Bead Width (in inches)

Bead 1	$\frac{1}{2}$
Bead 2	$\frac{1}{4}$
Bead 3	$\frac{3}{4}$
Bead 4	1
Bead 5	$\frac{1}{4}$
Bead 6	$\frac{3}{4}$

Alya started making this line plot. Draw Xs on the line plot to represent all 6 bead widths in the table.

Bead Width (in inches)

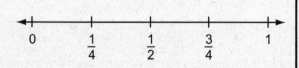

33 Sarah bought 6 packs of stickers. Then her sister gave her 9 more stickers. Now Sarah has 45 stickers.

Part A

How many stickers were in each pack?

(A) 6

(B) 9

(C) 15

(D) 30

Part B

How many stickers would Sarah have in all if her sister gave her 2 more packs of stickers?

_____

34 Karl is planting a garden. He has a total of 24 seeds. He plans to plant all the seeds in 4 rows with the same number of seeds in each row.

- How many seeds will Karl plant in each row?

- A friend suggests using 5 equal rows with the same number of seeds in each row. Explain the error in the friend's reasoning.

- Find another number of rows that Karl could use to plant the seeds with the same number of seeds in each row.

Write your answer in the space provided. Explain your answer using words, numbers, and/or symbols.

35 An art teacher needs 200 crayons for her class. The crayons come in boxes of 8, and she has 19 boxes. She also has a container of 42 individual crayons. She decides she will have enough crayons for her class.

- Is she correct? Why or why not?

- If she is correct, determine how many extra crayons she has, and explain why. If she is not correct, determine how many more crayons she will need, and explain why.

Write your answer in the space provided. Explain your answer using words, numbers, and/or symbols.

36 A business owner wants to rent a new office. The floor plan for the office is shown below.

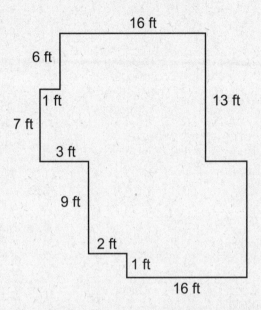

16 ft

6 ft

1 ft

13 ft

7 ft

3 ft

9 ft

2 ft

1 ft

16 ft

- The business owner says that the area of the office can be found by multiplying the length of the figure by the width of the figure. What is the error in this reasoning?

- What strategy would you advise the business owner to use to calculate the area of the office based on the floor plan given?

- Use that strategy to calculate the area of the office and explain your reasoning.

Write your answer in the space provided. Explain your answer using words, numbers, and/or symbols.

This page intentionally
left blank.

1 Solve.

$36 \div 6 = \boxed{}$

Ⓐ 6   Ⓒ 30

Ⓑ 7   Ⓓ 42

2 The students at Cherrywood Elementary are planting a vegetable garden. They divide a rectangular plot into 6 equal parts. The students plant 4 kinds of vegetables. The vegetables take up 1 or 2 parts of the plot, as shown in the table.

1 Part	2 Parts
lettuce	cucumbers
carrots	broccoli

Which of the following represents the fractional area of the vegetable garden taken up by lettuce and broccoli?

Select **all** the correct answers.

Ⓐ $\frac{1}{6}$

Ⓑ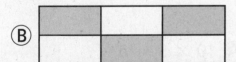

Ⓒ $\frac{3}{6}$

Ⓓ 3

3 Find the missing factor. $\boxed{} \times 9 = 72$

4 The table below shows the schedule for Keisha's summer camp.

Activity	Start Time	End Time
Lunch	12:05 p.m.	12:45 p.m.
Art	12:45 p.m.	2:00 p.m.
Theater	2:10 p.m.	3:50 p.m.
Swimming	4:15 p.m.	5:05 p.m.

Which activity takes the **LEAST** time?

(A) lunch   (C) theater

(B) art   (D) swimming

5 Carla has 7 packs of cards with 6 cards each. She gives some cards to Ranju. Carla has 36 cards now. How many cards does she give to Ranju?

6 What is the value of 732 − 256?

(A) 988   (C) 576

(B) 586   (D) 476

7 The array shows the beads Eliana is using to make a necklace.

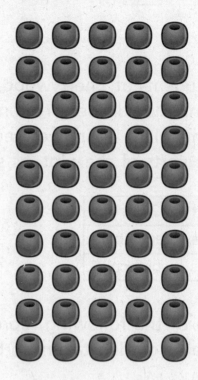

Select **all** the equations that can be used to find how many beads Eliana uses.

(A) $10 \times 5 = b$

(B) $b = 2 \times 5 \times 5$

(C) $b = 5 \times 5$

(D) $b = 10 + 5$

(E) $b \div 10 = 5$

8 Mr. Becker's class voted on their favorite subjects. Some of the results are shown on the graph.

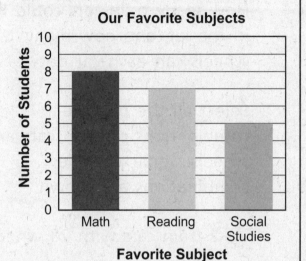

Our Favorite Subjects

Number of Students / Favorite Subject

Three more students voted for science than for social studies. Two fewer students voted for art than for science. How many students voted for art?

Ⓐ 3   Ⓒ 6

Ⓑ 5   Ⓓ 8

9 Shade a fraction of the whole model that makes the inequality true.

$$\frac{2}{6} < \boxed{} < \frac{4}{6}$$

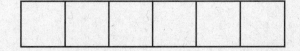

10 Which multiplication equation can be used to solve

42 ÷ 6 = ☐ ?

Fill in the blanks with the correct answers from the list.

_____ × 6 = _____

| 7 | 8 | 15 | 42 |

11 What do the missing numbers in the table have in common?

Select **all** that apply.

×	0	1	2	3	4	5	6	7	8	9	10
0	0	0	0	0	0	0	0	0	0	0	0
1	0	1	2	3	4	5	6	7	8	9	10
2	0	2	4	6	8	10		14	16	18	20
3	0	3	6	9	12	15	18	21	24	27	30
4	0	4	8	12	16	20	24	28	32	36	40
5	0	5	10	15	20	25		35	40	45	50
6	0	6	12	18	24	30		42	48	54	60
7	0	7	14	21	28	35		49	56	63	70
8	0	8	16	24	32	40	48	56	64	72	80
9	0	9	18	27	36	45		63	72	81	90
10	0	10	20	30	40	50	60	70	80	90	100

Ⓐ They are all odd numbers.

Ⓑ They are all even numbers.

Ⓒ They are all double the numbers to the right.

Ⓓ They are all 6 greater than the numbers above.

Ⓔ They are odd and even numbers.

12 Louisa builds a front deck that is 5 feet wide and 6 feet long. She wants to build a back deck with the same area but a different perimeter.

What could the dimensions of the back deck be?

Fill in the blanks with the correct numbers from the list on each side of the model.

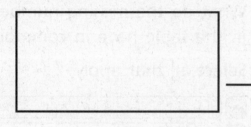

| 3 | 5 | 6 | 10 |

13 Maddie is building a model train. Each train car gets an equal number of wheels. There are 56 wheels in the kit. How many train cars could be in the kit, and how many wheels can each car get?

Select **all** the possible combinations of train cars and wheels. Some possible combinations are shown.

(A) 2 train cars with 28 wheels each

(B) 7 train cars with 8 wheels each

(C) 4 train cars with 12 wheels each

(D) 5 train cars with 6 wheels each

(E) 14 train cars with 4 wheels each

14 Mr. Garcia plans a garden plot. A model of the plot is shown below.

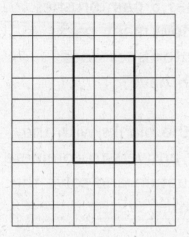

He then plans a second plot that has an area that is 3 times larger but with the same width as the first plot.

Fill in the blanks with the correct numbers from the list.

The length of the second plot is _____ times the length of the first plot, and its area is _____ square units.

3	5	15
15	32	45

15 What is 443 rounded to the nearest ten?

Ⓐ 400   Ⓒ 450

Ⓑ 440   Ⓓ 500

16 Three students ran around the school track. The table shows the part of 1 mile that two of the students ran.

Student	Part of Mile
Mila	$\frac{1}{2}$
Devon	
Cole	$\frac{3}{4}$

Devon ran farther than Mila, but not as far as Cole. Plot and label points on the number line to show the part of 1 mile that each student ran.

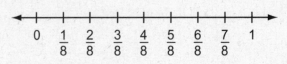

17 Marcus asks 25 students to vote for a favorite color. The table shows some of the results.

Color	Number of Students
Red	6
Blue	9
Green	5
Yellow	

Create a bar graph to show the number of students who voted for each of the 4 colors.

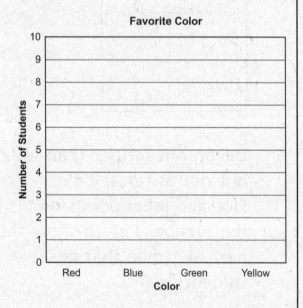

18 Hannah has some packs of paintbrushes. She has 30 paintbrushes in all. Each pack has 6 paintbrushes in it. How many packs of paintbrushes does Hannah have?

Fill in the blanks with the correct answers to complete the equation and solve the problem.

_____ ÷ _____ = _____
packs of paintbrushes

19 Which expression has the same product as 3 × 80?

Ⓐ 4 × 70   Ⓒ 5 × 30

Ⓑ 6 × 40   Ⓓ 8 × 50

20 Which shape can never be a square?

Ⓐ parallelogram

Ⓑ rectangle

Ⓒ rhombus

Ⓓ trapezoid

21 What is the value of the missing number?

$$8 \times 6 = (8 \times 2) + (8 \times \boxed{})$$

(A) 2

(B) 4

(C) 6

(D) 8

22 Bryan is measuring his bedroom. It has a perimeter of 48 feet. What could the side lengths for Bryan's bedroom be?

Fill in the blanks with the correct answers from the list.

_____ feet long, _____ feet wide

6	8	10	14

23 A part of a multiplication pattern is shown.

Part A

Fill in the 2 blanks with the correct numbers to complete the table.

x	1	2	3	4	5	6	7	8
5	5	10	15	20	___	30	___	40
	odd	even	odd	even	?	even	odd	

Part B

Would the question mark in the bottom row of the table (below the 5) be even or odd?

The question mark in the bottom row should state odd/even because an odd/even number times an odd number will be an odd/even number.

24 Grayson and Sophie have containers that are the same size.

Grayson has 8 liters (L) of water in his container. Sophie does not know how much water is in her container. About how much more water in liters does Sophie have than Grayson?

Grayson   **Sophie**

---

25 Mai divides the shape below into equal-sized parts like the one shown.

What fraction of the shape does the shaded part show?

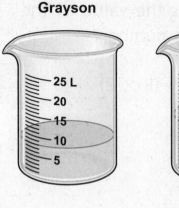

(A) 1

(C) $\frac{1}{5}$

(B) 5

(D) $\frac{1}{6}$

---

26 Maddie has 5 bags. Each bag has 8 apple slices.

Which expression can she use to find the total number of apple slices?

(A) 8 − 5

(C) 8 × 5

(B) 8 ÷ 5

(D) 8 + 5

© Houghton Mifflin Harcourt Publishing Company

27 Which of the following is **greater** than $\frac{1}{2}$?

Select **all** the correct answers.

Ⓐ $\frac{1}{3}$

Ⓓ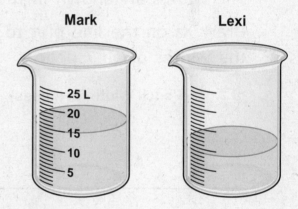

0   B   1

Ⓑ $\frac{4}{8}$

Ⓔ $\frac{3}{8}$

Ⓒ $\frac{3}{2}$

---

28 Which multiplication fact can help you solve the expression 54 ÷ 6?

Ⓐ 6 × 4   Ⓒ 5 × 4

Ⓑ 9 × 6   Ⓓ 5 × 9

---

29 Josh drew a model of his mom's office on paper with unit squares.

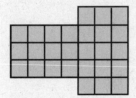

What expression can be used to help find the area of the office?

(_____ × _____) +

(_____ × _____)

---

30 Lexi and Mark have containers that are the same size.

Mark   Lexi

25 L
20
15
10
5

Mark has 15 liters (L) of water in his container. Lexi does not know how much water is in her container. About how much less water in liters does Lexi have than Mark?

Ⓐ 6 L   Ⓒ 15 L

Ⓑ 9 L   Ⓓ 24 L

31 Which fraction is represented by the length between point *A* and point *B* on the number line?

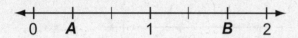

Ⓐ $\frac{1}{3}$ Ⓒ $\frac{4}{3}$

Ⓑ $\frac{2}{3}$ Ⓓ $\frac{5}{3}$

32 Janine measured the width of 7 pencils. The widths are shown in the table.

Draw Xs on the line plot to represent the widths of all 7 pencils.

Pencil Width (in inches)

Pencil Width (in inches)	
Pencil 1	$\frac{1}{2}$
Pencil 2	$\frac{1}{4}$
Pencil 3	$\frac{3}{4}$
Pencil 4	1
Pencil 5	$\frac{1}{4}$
Pencil 6	$\frac{3}{4}$
Pencil 7	$\frac{3}{4}$

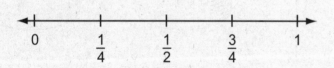

33 On Friday the students sold 55 tickets to their school play. On Saturday the students sold 95 tickets. Their goal is to sell 250 tickets by Sunday. How many more tickets do the students need to sell to meet their goal?

_____

34 An art teacher wishes to display 36 pieces of student artwork in the community. She wants to display the pieces equally across 4 different locations.

- How many pieces will the art teacher display at each location?

- A friend suggests that all the pieces be displayed at 5 different locations with the same number of pieces at each location. Explain the error in the friend's reasoning.

- As part of your explanation, find another number of locations the art teacher could display all the pieces of student artwork with an equal number of pieces at each location.

Write your answer in the space provided. Explain your answer using words, numbers, and/or symbols.

35 Penny is planning a party and needs 150 balloons. The balloons come in packages of 9, and she has 13 packages. She also has 25 balloons left over from another party. She decides she will have enough balloons for the party.

- Is she correct? Why or why not?

- If she is correct, determine how many extra balloons she has, and explain why. If she is not correct, determine how many more balloons she will need, and explain why.

Write your answer in the space provided. Explain your answer using words, numbers, and/or symbols.

36 A city is planning to build a new park. The planned dimensions of the park are shown below.

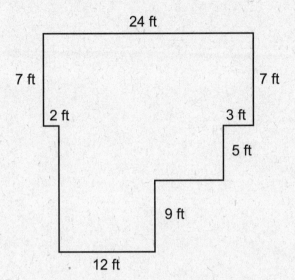

- One of the park planners says that the area of the park can be found by multiplying the lengths of the longest sides. What is the error in this reasoning?

- What strategy would you advise the planner to use to calculate the area of the park based on the image given?

- Use that strategy to calculate the area of the park and explain your reasoning.

Write your answer in the space provided. Explain your answer using words, numbers, and/or symbols.

This page intentionally
left blank.

1 What is the value of 7×8?

Ⓐ 49   Ⓒ 58

Ⓑ 56   Ⓓ 64

2 Figure A shows $\frac{1}{4}$ of the whole shaded.

Figure A:

Figure B:

Which fraction of the whole is shaded in Figure B?

Ⓐ $\frac{1}{6}$ Ⓒ $\frac{6}{1}$

Ⓑ $\frac{4}{6}$ Ⓓ $\frac{6}{4}$

3 What is the unknown number in the equation below?

$4 = \boxed{} \div 7$

4 Millicent shovels snow in the morning, afternoon, and evening.

Fill in the missing start time, end time, and time spent shoveling in the table.

	Start Time	End Time	Time Spent Shoveling
Morning	6:54 a.m.	: a.m.	20 minutes
Afternoon	: p.m.	3:45 p.m.	16 minutes
Evening	7:48 p.m.	8:01 p.m.	minutes

5 A school receives a shipment of 9 boxes of textbooks. Each box has 8 textbooks. The school expects to receive a total of 110 textbooks. How many more textbooks should the school receive?

Ⓐ 38   Ⓒ 72

Ⓑ 48   Ⓓ 93

6 What is the value of $591 - 188$?

7 Marisol has 54 marbles. She places an equal number of marbles in each of 6 cups. She then gives 3 of the cups to her friend. How many marbles does she give to her friend?

Ⓐ 12   Ⓒ 36

Ⓑ 27   Ⓓ 51

8 Gino's school is open for 19 days in January. The school is open for 15 days in February. In March the school is open for 5 more days than in February.

Draw a bar graph to show the correct number of days the school is open each month.

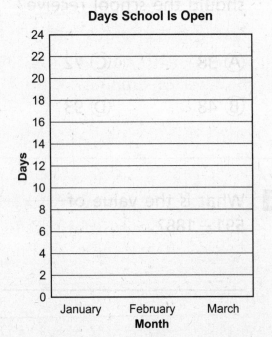

9 A fraction model for $\frac{2}{3}$ is shown.

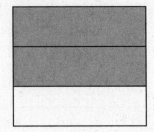

Kerri claims that an equivalent fraction is $\frac{4}{6}$. Which statement describes whether she is correct?

Ⓐ Yes, because splitting each part of the model into 2 pieces shows equivalence.

Ⓑ Yes, because splitting each part of the model into 3 pieces shows equivalence.

Ⓒ No, because $\frac{2}{3}$ and $\frac{4}{6}$ will have different numbers of shaded parts.

Ⓓ No, because $\frac{2}{3}$ and $\frac{4}{6}$ will have different numbers of total parts.

10 Write a multiplication equation that is equivalent to $42 \div 6 = $ ⬜ .

11 Which statement is true about the multiplication table?

×	0	1	2	3	4	5	6	7	8	9	10
0	0	0	0	0	0	0	0	0	0	0	0
1	0	1	2	3	4	5	6	7	8	9	10
2	0	2	4	6	8	10	12	14	16	18	20
3	0	3	6	9	12	15	18	21	24	27	30
4	0	4	8	12	16	20	24	28	32	36	40

Ⓐ Every other row will have only odd numbers because in the odd-numbered rows any number times an odd number will always be an odd number.

Ⓑ Every other row will have only odd numbers because in the odd-numbered rows an odd number times an odd number will always be an odd number.

Ⓒ Every other row will have only even numbers because in the even-numbered rows any number times an even number will always be an even number.

Ⓓ Every other row will have only even numbers because in the even-numbered rows an even number times an even number will always be an even number.

12 A rectangle has a width of 4 inches and a length of 9 inches. Which of these rectangles has the same perimeter but a smaller area than the rectangle described?

Ⓐ a rectangle with a width of 5 inches and a length of 8 inches

Ⓑ a rectangle with a width of 6 inches and a length of 6 inches

Ⓒ a rectangle with a width of 9 inches and a length of 4 inches

Ⓓ a rectangle with a width of 10 inches and a length of 3 inches

13 Nathan has 12 oranges. He places the oranges into 3 bags so that each bag has the same number of oranges.

Complete an equation to show the number of oranges in each bag.

Fill in the blanks with the correct answers from the list.

_____ ÷ _____ = _____

2	3	4	6	12

14 A figure is shown.

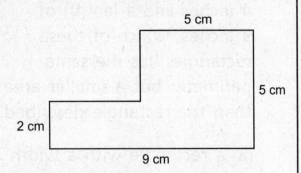

5 cm

5 cm

2 cm

9 cm

Alison says that the area of the figure can be found by $5 \times 5 + 2 \times 9$.

Which of these statements explains whether Alison is correct?

Ⓐ Alison is correct, so the area is 43 square centimeters.

Ⓑ Alison is incorrect because she counted the overlapping area twice.

Ⓒ Alison is incorrect because she should have added the side lengths of each rectangle, not multiplied them together.

Ⓓ Alison is incorrect because she should have multiplied the areas of the two rectangles together, not added them together.

15 The table shows the number of students in each of four schools.

School	Number of Students
School A	337
School B	451
School C	345
School D	418

Part A

Round the number of students in each school to the nearest ten.

School	Number of Students	Number of Students Rounded to Nearest Ten
School A	337	
School B	451	
School C	345	
School D	418	

Part B

Which school has a number of students that rounds to 400 when rounded to the nearest hundred?

Ⓐ School A   Ⓒ School C

Ⓑ School B   Ⓓ School D

16 Amelia eats $\frac{3}{4}$ of a pie. Yolanda eats $\frac{3}{3}$ of a different pie.

Amelia's Pie   **Yolanda's Pie**

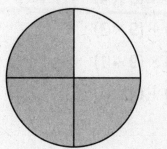

Which statement is true?

Ⓐ Amelia must have eaten a larger amount of pie, because $\frac{3}{3} < \frac{3}{4}$.

Ⓑ Yolanda must have eaten a larger amount of pie, because $\frac{3}{4} < \frac{3}{3}$.

Ⓒ The amount of pie eaten by the two girls cannot be compared because the denominators are different.

Ⓓ The amount of pie eaten by the two girls cannot be compared because the fractions refer to different wholes.

17 The bar graph shows the number of visitors at a museum on Friday, Saturday, and Sunday.

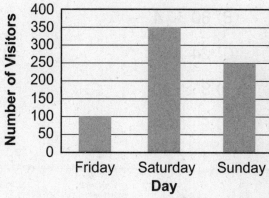

How many more visitors does the museum have on Saturday and Sunday than on Friday?

Ⓐ 200

Ⓑ 500

Ⓒ 600

Ⓓ 700

18 Leah has some baskets of apples. She has 27 apples in all. Each basket has 9 apples in it. How many baskets of apples does Leah have?

Fill in the blanks with the correct answers to complete the equation.

_____ ÷ _____ = _____ baskets of apples

19 Select **all** the expressions that have the same product as 4 × 60.

Ⓐ 3 × 40

Ⓑ 80 × 4

Ⓒ 24 × 1

Ⓓ 8 × 30

Ⓔ 6 × 40

20 A rectangle and a rhombus are shown.

Select **all** the attributes these shapes always have in common.

Ⓐ number of angles

Ⓑ number of sides

Ⓒ number of parallel sides

Ⓓ number of acute angles

Ⓔ number of right angles

21 Which expression is equivalent to 9 × 8?

Ⓐ (9 × 5) + (9 × 4)

Ⓑ (9 × 5) + (9 × 3)

Ⓒ (9 + 8) × (9 + 1)

Ⓓ (4 × 5) + (4 × 4)

22 Lori's bedroom has a perimeter of 48 feet.

Select **all** the shapes that could represent her bedroom.

Ⓐ
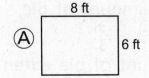
8 ft
6 ft

Ⓑ
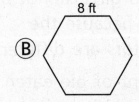
8 ft

Ⓒ
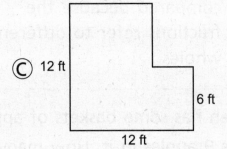
8 ft
12 ft
6 ft
12 ft

Ⓓ
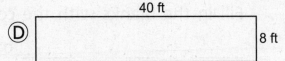
40 ft
8 ft

23 A multiplication table is shown.

×	0	1	2	3	4	5	6	7	8	9	10
0	0	0	0	0	0	0	0	0	0	0	0
1	0	1	2	3	4	5	6	7	8	9	10
2	0	2	4	6	8	10	12	14	16	18	20
3	0	3	6	9	12	15	18	21	24	27	30
4	0	4	8	12	16	20	24	28	32	36	40
5	0	5	10	15	20	25	30	35	40	45	50
6	0	6	12	18	24	30	36	42	48	54	60
7	0	7	14	21	28	35	42	49	56	63	70
8	0	8	16	24	32	40	48	56	64	72	80
9	0	9	18	27	36	45	54	63	72	81	90
10	0	10	20	30	40	50	60	70	80	90	100

Which statement correctly describes how to find the multiples of 4 in the multiplication table?

Ⓐ Find all the numbers that start with 4.

Ⓑ Find all the numbers that end with 4.

Ⓒ Find all the shaded numbers that would meet at an unshaded 4.

Ⓓ Find all the numbers in the same row or column as a shaded 4.

24 Sarah and Josh have the same size containers, as shown.

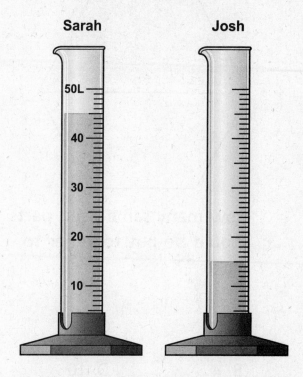

Sarah has 45 liters (L) of water in her container. Josh does not know how much water is in his container.

About how much more water in liters does Sarah have than Josh?

_____

25 The shaded part represents $\frac{1}{2}$.

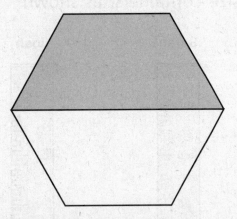

How many same-sized parts
should be put together to
make $\frac{8}{2}$?

Ⓐ 2   Ⓒ 8

Ⓑ 4   Ⓓ 10

26 Anna has 4 vases. Each vase
has 8 flowers in it. How many
flowers does Anna have?

Ⓐ 2   Ⓒ 12

Ⓑ 4   Ⓓ 32

27 Shade the model to show a
fraction of the whole model
that makes the inequality true.

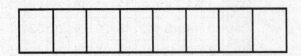

28 What number will make BOTH
of these equations true?

$3 \times \underline{\quad\quad} = 15$

$15 \div 3 = \underline{\quad\quad}$

29 The students in Ms. Kelly's class are creating a reading space for the classroom. They draw this model of the space.

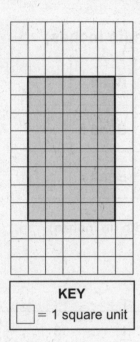

KEY

☐ = 1 square unit

Part A

Write an equation to find the area of the reading space.

_____

Part B

Ms. Kelly decides to make another space in the classroom for art supplies. It will be half the area of the reading space. Which of these are possible dimensions?

Select the **two** correct answers.

Ⓐ 4 × 5   Ⓓ 2 × 40

Ⓑ 2 × 10   Ⓔ 4 × 8

Ⓒ 8 × 5

---

30 Shawna and Nicky have different amounts of liquid, as shown.

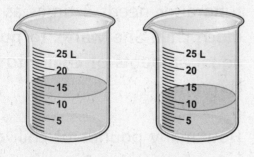

They both pour their liquid into a bigger empty container. What is the volume of liquid in the bigger container?

Ⓐ 4 L   Ⓑ 8 L   Ⓒ 12 L   Ⓓ 20 L

31 Logan has a box for beads. It is divided into 6 equal parts, as shown.

red	red	blue
purple	pink	orange

Which number line shows the part of the box filled with red beads?

Ⓐ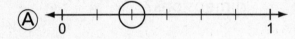

Ⓑ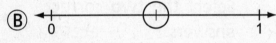

Ⓒ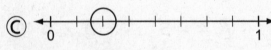

Ⓓ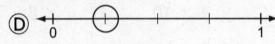

32 Amit measured the size of several beads. The widths are shown in the table. Draw Xs on the line plot to represent all 6 bead widths in the table.

Bead Width (in inches)

Bead 1	$\frac{1}{2}$	Bead 4	1
Bead 2	$\frac{1}{4}$	Bead 5	$\frac{1}{4}$
Bead 3	$\frac{1}{2}$	Bead 6	$\frac{1}{2}$

Beads Width (in inches)

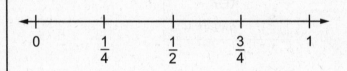

33 Ms. Potter is making her famous chili for a fundraiser. She makes 8 pounds of chili. She then gets a call that the fundraiser needs 3 times as much chili. She wants to put equal amounts of chili into 6 containers.

How many pounds of chili are in each container?

_____

34 A basketball team of 20 players is running a drill. The coach assigns the players to 5 equal groups.

- How many players does the coach assign to each group?

- A player suggests that the team be assigned to 6 equal groups. Explain the error in the player's reasoning.

- As part of your explanation, find another number of equal groups to which the coach could assign the players.

Write your answer in the space provided. Explain your answer using words, numbers, and/or symbols.

35 Jim is saving money to buy a bicycle that costs $90. He already has $12. He plans on saving $4 a week for the next 19 weeks. He estimates that he will have enough money to buy the bicycle.

- Is he correct? Why or why not?

- If he is correct, determine how much extra money he will have, and explain why. If he is not correct, determine how much more money he will need, and explain why.

Write your answer in the space provided. Explain your answer using words, numbers, and/or symbols.

36 An architect plans to add a porch onto a house and gives the builders plans to follow. The plans for the porch are shown.

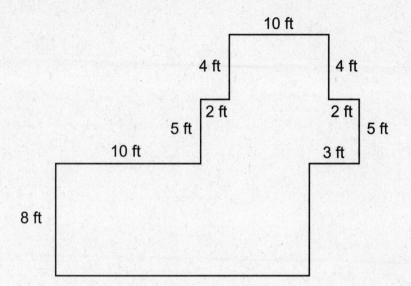

- One of the builders says that the area of the porch can be found by multiplying the lengths of longest sides. What is the error in this reasoning?

- What strategy would you advise the builder to use to calculate the area of the porch based on the image given?

- Use that strategy to calculate the area of the porch and explain your reasoning.

Write your answer in the space provided. Explain your answer using words, numbers, and/or symbols.